ISRAELI KIDS' LETTERS TO TERRORISTS

Developed & Compiled by
JOHN SHUCHART

Cover and Book Design by Jonathan Dickson & Steve Scearcy
Photography by Kelly Levy

Published by The Shuchart Foundation
11401 Brookwood
Leawood, KS 66211

First Edition copyright© 2008 by John Shuchart
Revised Edition copyright© 2011 by John Shuchart

Third Printing, August, 2012

ISBN: 978-0-615-21057-5

No part of this book may be used, stored in a retrieval system, reproduced or transmitted in any form by any means, electronic, digital, mechanical, photocopying, recording, or otherwise whatsoever without written permission from the publisher, except in the case of brief quotations embodied in critical articles and reviews. For further information, contact:

The Shuchart Foundation
913.485.3336
john@jshuchart.com

Website: www.israelikidsletterstoterrorists.com

Printed in United States of America

Dedicated to
IRENA SENDLER

and

Those Supporting the State of Israel
and the Jewish People.

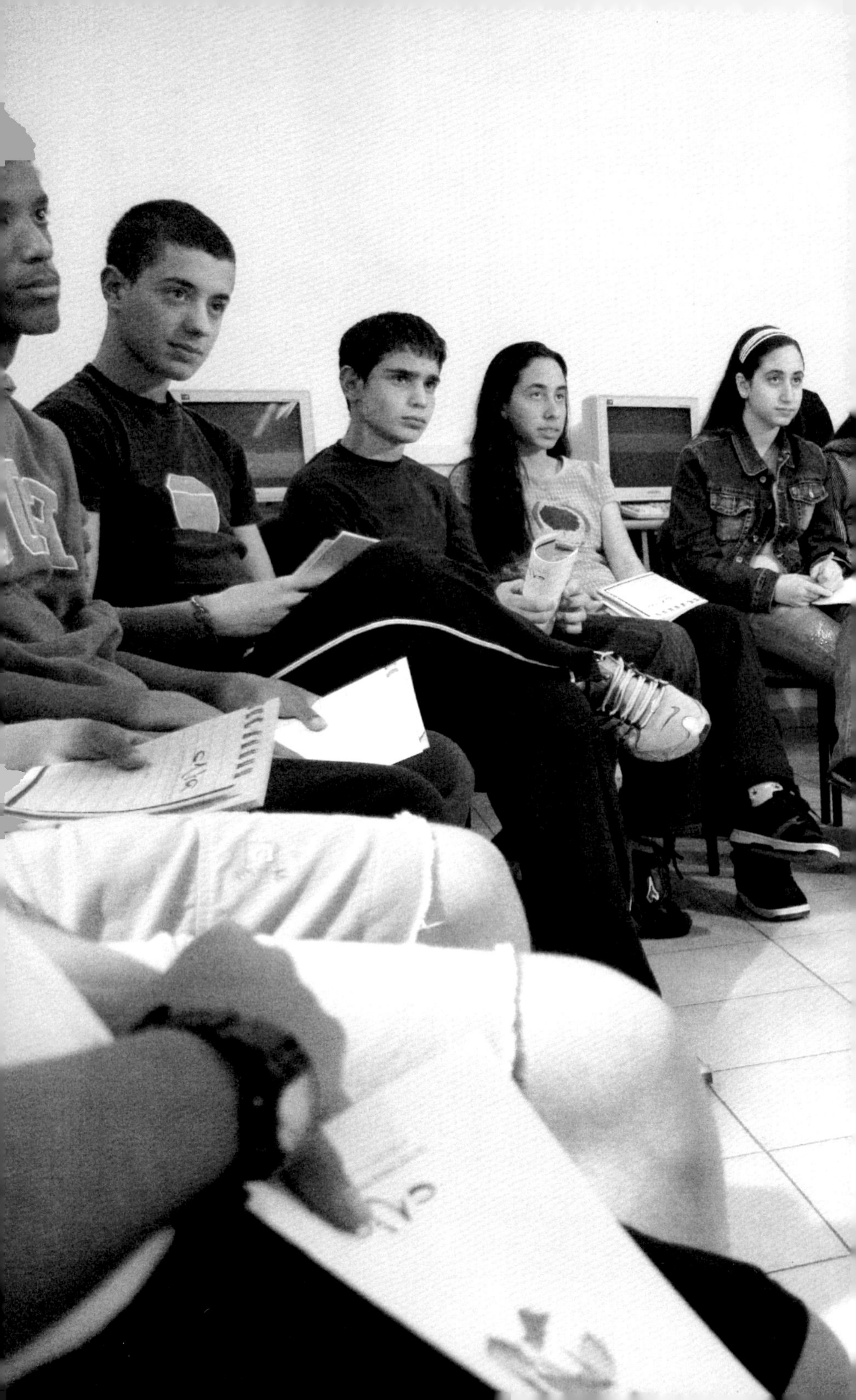

Table of Contents

Foreword by Israeli President Shimon Peres 7

Introduction of Irena Sendler 9

Introduction 11

Israeli Kids' Letters To Terrorists (excerpts) 15

The Irena Sendler Story 110

Acknowledgements 121

Special Thank-You 124

About the Editor 125

Descriptions of Students' Home Cities 126

Guest Speaker Opportunities 127

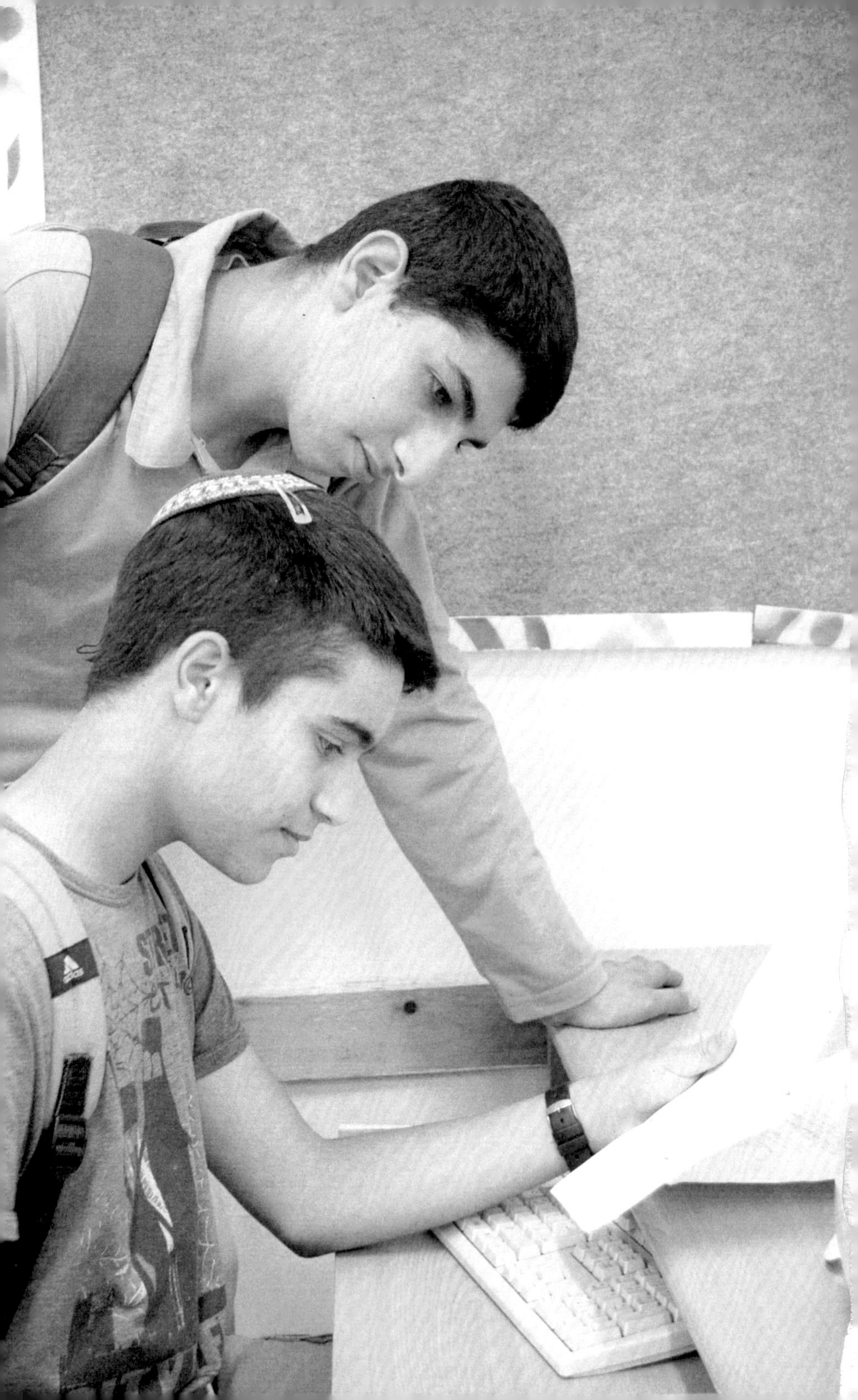

Foreword

THE PRESIDENT

Jerusalem

Dear Reader,

The target of relentless terrorist attacks, this collection of letters written by Israeli schoolchildren – Arab and Jewish – could not better express the yearning of these children for a long-term hiatus in the constant threat of terrorism to which they, and their families, are exposed.

This unique project allows the children to voice their inner feelings, each from their own personal perspective, and address the terrorists who have caused havoc with their lives. They seek to probe the motivation that causes a human being to abandon his or her humanity and turn into a device that disseminates destruction and grief. They are keen to understand the rationale that breeds such hatred, the people who choose death over life.

Working together, these young Jewish and Arab children have broken down the barriers of prejudice and intolerance, substituting age-old conflicts by a spirit of partnership in the quest for a better world. Destined to assume the mantle of responsibility for our society and become tomorrow's leaders, these meaningful letters serve as a tangible message of peace that must fall on fertile soil if we are to start building a future of hope for these children today.

Sincerely,

Shimon Peres

www.israelikidsletterstoterrorists.com

ANOTHER "THE STUDENT AS THE CUSTOMER" SUCCESS STORY:
THE DISCOVERY OF IRENA SENDLER

"To Save A Child, is to Save the World"----Jewish Talmud

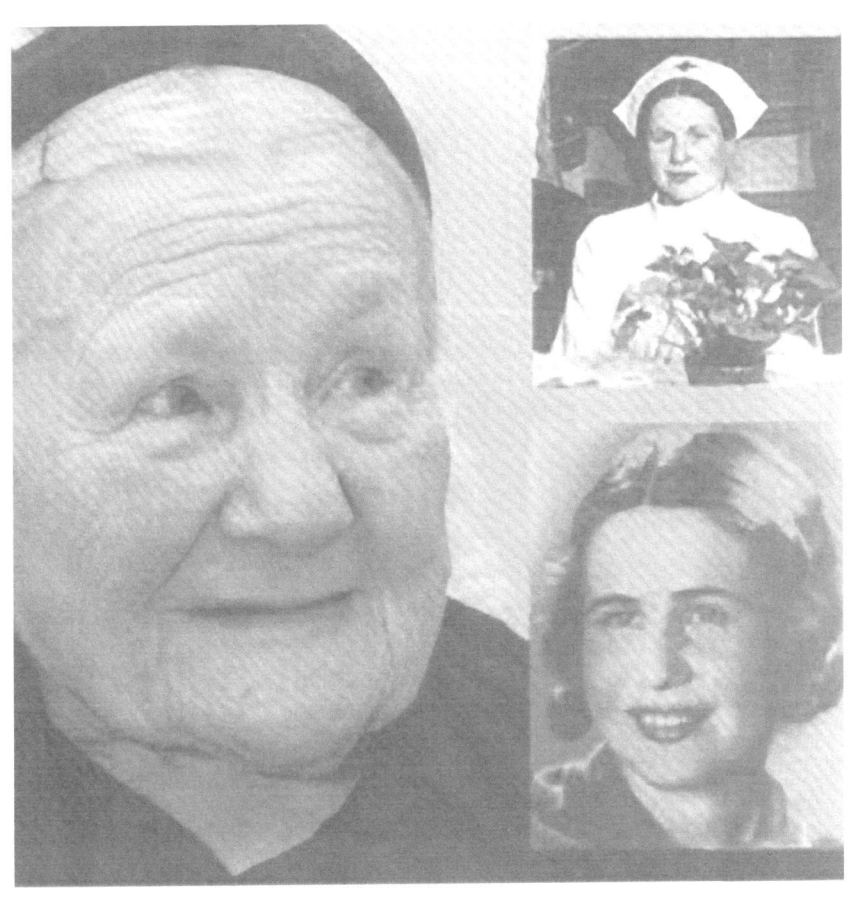

You'll find Irena's incredible story and how it was uncovered by students beginning on page 110.

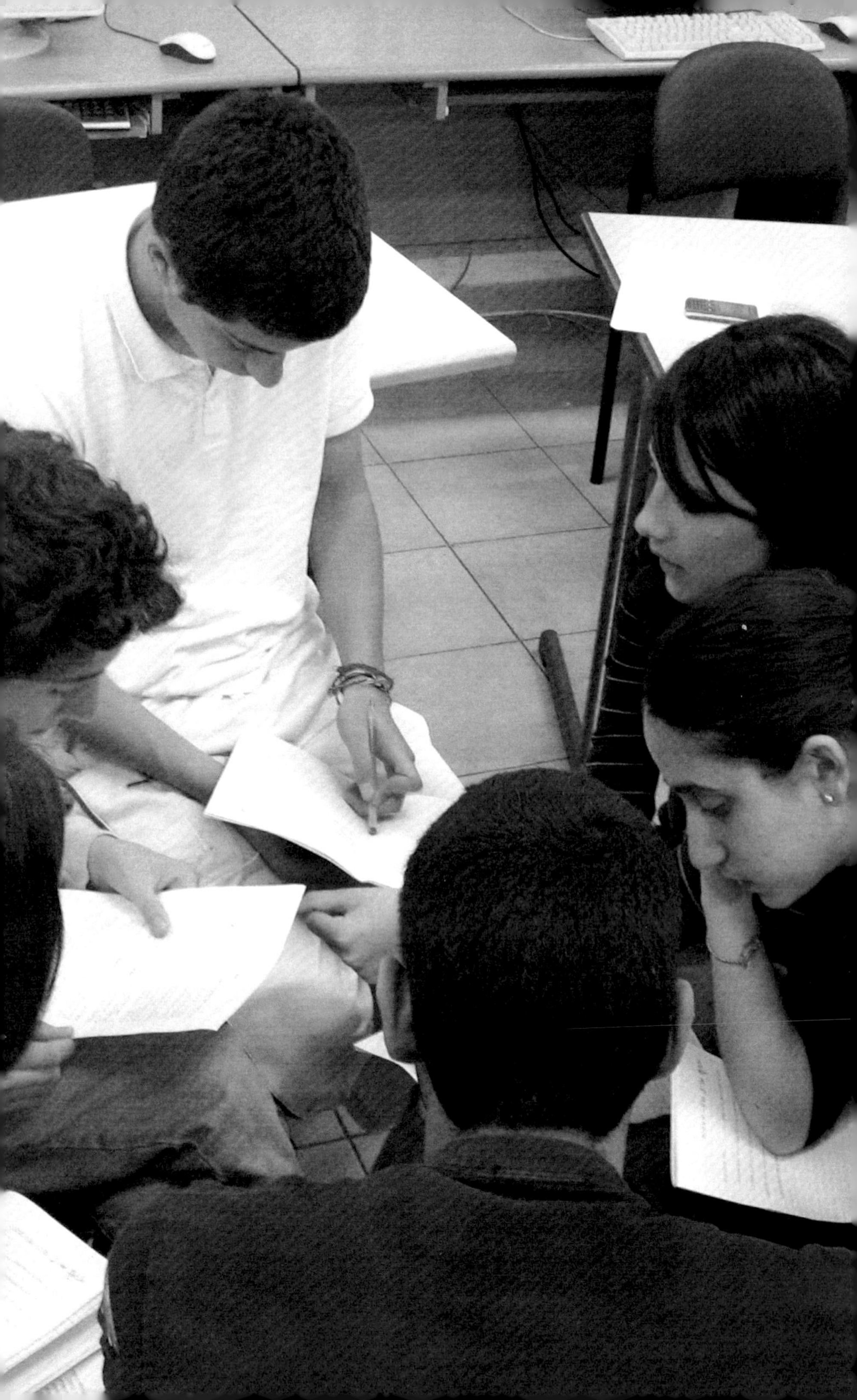

Introduction

"We maintain that there is no excuse for acts of terrorism against Israel and that Israel has the same right as every other nation to defend her citizens from such violent attacks ."

Pastor John Hagee, Founder and National Chairman, Christians United for Israel

This is the second time I have compiled and edited letters written to terrorists by students in their teens. The first book, *Kids' Letters to Terrorists*, resulted from a course taken by seventh and eighth graders living in the central part of the United States. Most of these students had only experienced terrorism vicariously, watching and reading about the horrors of the September 11, 2001 attacks in the United States.

This time the students were Israeli high school students, many of whom face terrorism in their cities almost every day. And as exciting as the idea to put together a book of letters from Israeli teenagers (who wouldn't want to hear what Israeli kids have to say about terrorism?), the project almost didn't take place. When I was first approached by the Israelis and explained the concept to them, their immediate response was "Our students already know about terrorism. They don't need to create a course, they just need to write the letters." I told them that if that was true, then they didn't need me. They first had to gather up some students, put them in front of computers, and have them write letters.

I assumed the project was dead, but eventually I received a phone call from Israel telling me they had decided to move forward, having kids create the course, implementing it in high schools across the country, and putting together a book comprised of the most compelling letters. Why the turnaround? The adults had discovered that even though many of the students have experienced terrorism (some with rockets landing very short distances from them), very few have ever shared their real fears and feelings. Adults thought their kids were dealing well with the terrorism, but when they actually sat down and talked with teenagers, they discovered that teens don't think it's "cool" to talk about terrorism with their friends. And parents and teachers? Not a chance! So most of the students have held in their emotions. A course created by students for students would create the environment needed to help these kids share their feelings with each other.

Introduction (cont.)

Once the Israelis decided to move forward, we opened up the throttle. I went to Israel for seven days, met with teachers (25) and then with students (10) from several cities in the country.

Three of the ten students who helped create WRITTEN are Arab Israelis. Each student is enrolled in an after school project (Net@) involving computer repair and networking. Each class has two instructors, one of whom is in essence a social worker. In order to attend class, students are required to do community service work. In some cities, this requirement is fulfilled when Net@ opens computer repair spaces. Community members may bring their computers to the students who will repair them for no charge. Net@ is one of several programs available to youth at risk through Israel's Youth Futures program. Students attend Net@ classes twice each week after school for four hours when they are in the ninth grade and once each week during their next three years of high school. Graduates typically have passed the very difficult examinations offered by CISCO Systems and Microsoft and as a result their futures are somewhat secure. Most will enter the Israeli army after high school graduation and thanks to their Net@ training, will be assigned to technological positions. Upon leaving the army, they find their skills very much in demand. Instead of being a youth at risk, students become a valuable asset to their families and their country.

Creating a course on terrorism with a mixed population (both Arab and Jewish Israelis) could have been a fragile undertaking. In the beginning, I anticipated that there would be heavy emotional outbursts from one side or the other. I remember gulping a few times before I got up the courage to ask one of the Arab students to describe a terrorist to the rest of the group. As he began to speak, my eyes bounced back and forth from him to a Jewish Israeli. I waited for something to be said that would raise the ire of the Jewish students; I imagined myself spending the remainder of the session pulling people off each other.

I couldn't have been more mistaken. These young people not only functioned well together, they enjoyed being together! I will never forget when one of the Jewish students walked over to an Arab student, put her arm around him and proudly proclaimed, "See...we like each other here. We don't have any problems with each other. We don't want to hurt each other. If you would just leave us kids alone, everything would be fine."

Introduction (cont.)

Kids think, if given the chance, they can begin the process of creating peace in the Middle East. Is this just youth spouting off? Possibly, but I don't think so. After having the opportunity to meet many of the students who participated in the WRITTEN course and to absorb the impact of their letters, I find myself being much more optimistic. The letters in this book show that students generally believe that terrorists can turn from their current courses of action and begin responding to reason and logic. Many of the students' letters express trust that there is a better way to handle conflict, offer creative suggestions for handling ideological differences, and at times even use humor in an attempt to diffuse the terrorists' anger.

Trust in the future, creativity, and humor are traits of resilient people. I believe that it is the natural resilience of many of these students that enables them to withstand the threat of terrorism that is present in their daily lives and to project onto terrorists their faith that the terrorists can withstand the negative influences present in their own lives.

John Shuchart
john@jshuchart.com
www.israelikidsletterstoterrorists.com
913.485.3336
June, 2011

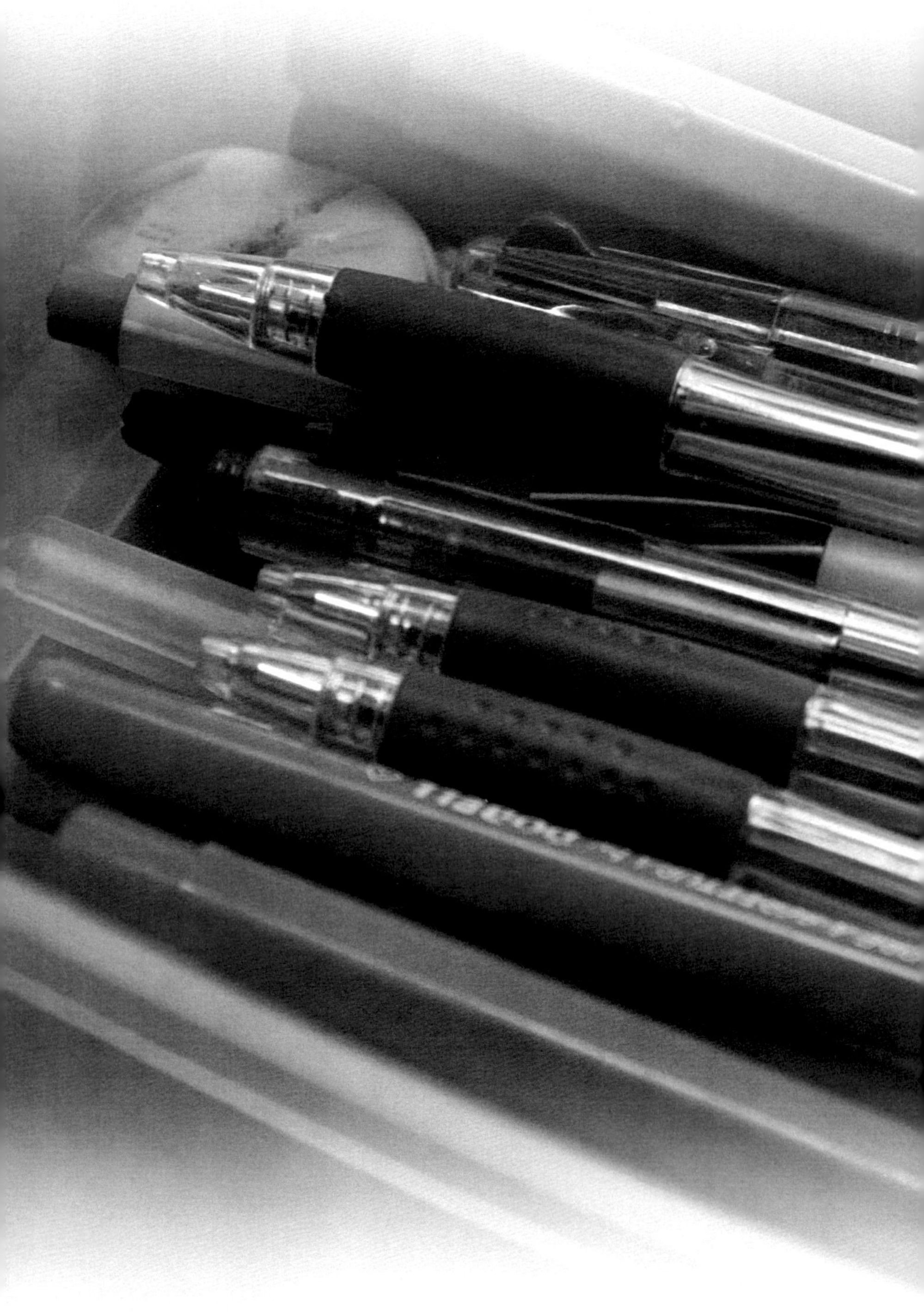

I live in Sderot and am constantly fearful because of you. How would you react if rockets were falling all around you non-stop? How would you respond if you didn't feel protected even in your home? If your children couldn't go out to play? I hope that someday we'll manage to live together in peace.

Diana, 11th grade, Sderot

אני גרה בשדרות ונמצאת במצב של פחד מתמיד בגללך, איך אתה היית מגיב אם מסביבך היו נופלים טילים בלי הפסקה? איך אתה מגיב אם אפילו בבית לא היית מרגיש מוגן? אם הילדים שלך לא היו יכולים אפילו לצאת לשחק בחוץ? מקווה שיום אחד נצליח לחיות ביחד בשלום.

דיאנה, כיתה י"א, שדרות

أنا أسكن في سديروت وأعيش حالة دائمة من الخوف بسببك. ماذا سيكون رد فعلك إذا كانت تسقط من حولك صواريخ دون توقف؟ ماذا سيكون رد فعلك إذا لم تشعر محميًا حتى في بيتك؟ إذا لم يستطع أولادك حتى اللعب خارج البيت؟ إنني آمل أن في يوم من الأيام سنتمكن من التعايش السلمي.

ديانا, الصف الحادي عشر, سديروت

Perhaps I don't understand because I'm just a little girl. When I hear about a terrorist attack, the first thing I feel is anger, the second is sadness, but the third time it turns into emptiness and deep pain. I'm a volunteer who tries to help people when they feel sick. However, no ambulance, surgery or medicine could cure the pain one feels by the death of people you are close to. I really believe that everyone deserves a second chance, but the question is whether you're willing to take a second chance and use it to your advantage. I hope you could understand our side and our pain as well.

Linoy, 9th grade, Eilat

ואולי אני לא מבינה ואולי אני סתם ילדה קטנה אבל מה שאני כותבת לך עכשיו הוא אמיתי וכנה. כשאני שומעת על פיגוע הדבר הראשון שמרגישים הוא כעס בפעם השנייה זה עצב, בפעם השלישית זה הופך לריקנות וכאב עמוק.
אני מתנדבת מד"א ואני עוזרת לאנשים אני מטפלת בהם כשרע להם אבל שום אמבולנס ניתוח או תרופה יכול לרפא את הכאב שבמוות של אנשים שקרובים אליך.
אני באמת מאמינה שלכל אחד מגיע הזדמנות שנייה אבל השאלה היא אם אתה מוכן לקבל אותה ולנצל אותה.
אני מקווה שתוכל להבין גם את הצד שלנו ואת הכאב שלנו
לינוי, כיתה ט', אילת

علني لا أفهم, لعلني بنت صغيرة السن لا غير, ولكن ما أكتبه لك هو حقيقي وصريح. عندما أسمع بحدوث عملية إرهابية فاول شيء أشعر به هو الغضب, وفي المرة الثانية فينتابني الشعور بالحزن, أما في المرة الثالثة فيصبح الشعور شعوراً بالخواء والألم العميق إنني متطوعة في منظمة نجمة داوود الحمراء (ماذا – ما يشبه الهلال الأحمر عندكم) وأساعد الناس. أعالجهم في أوقات الشدة. ولكنه لا توجد أي سيارة إسعاف أو عملية جراحية أو دواء يمكنها شفاء الألم الناتج عن موت ناس قريبين منك أعتقد حقاً أن كل واحد يستحق أن تتاح لا فرصة ثانية, ولكن هل أنت مستعد لانتهاز هذه الفرصة؟
آمل بأنك ستستطيع إدراك طرفنا وألمنا أيضًا.
لينوي, الصف التاسع, إيلات

Go to www.alljobs.co.il. There are lots of job offers. Why did you choose a profession in which you have to kill dozens of innocent people? What did they offer you? Lots of money for your family? 72 virgins in heaven? This can be solved, too. Go to www.jdate.co.il. There are a lot of virgins there, waiting for a partner, more than 72. Today, with the internet, you can do anything.

Tal and Meidad, 12th grade, Ramle

יש שם מלא מודעות דרושים, מלא מקצועות www.AllJobs.co.il - תיכנס ל עבודה אחרים. למה דווקא בחרת במקצוע שאתה צריך להרוג בו עשרות אנשים חפים מפשע ובסוף למות בעצמך? מה הציעו לך? מלא כסף למשפחה? יש שם מלא www.JDate.co.il 72 בתולות בגן עדן? גם לזה יש פתרון, כנס ל בתולות שמחכות לבן זוג. יותר מ- 72. היום בעזרת האינטרנט אפשר לעשות הכול.

טל ומידד, כיתה י"ב, רמלה

على شبكة الإنترنت, تجد هناك الكثير من إعلانات www.AllJobs.co.il زر موقع "مطلوب", الكثير من الأعمال والوظائف الأخرى. لماذا اخترت بالذات مهنة يجب عليك في نطاقها قتل عشرات الأبرياء وفي النهاية تقتل أنت أيضًا؟ ما الذي عرضوه عليك؟ الأموال الطائلة لعائلتك؟ www.JDate.co.il 72 حورية في الجنة؟ لذلك أيضًا يوجد حلاً. زر موقع ال72-. تجد هناك الكثير من العذراوات اللواتي ينتظرن زوجًا. وعددهن يتجاوز. في أيامنا يمكننا أن نعمل كل شيء بمساعدة الإنترنت

تال وميداد, الصف الثاني عشر, الرملة

Israeli Kids' Letters to Terrorists

I would like to imagine that every time I watch the news and hear about a terrorist attack...they show in the background all the people that are shouting and crying, those who are trying with great effort and hope to find someone dear to them, a relative, a boy- friend or a girlfriend or even a stranger they saw just a second ago. I like to pretend all these people were actors on a set and the director would soon say "Cut!" and everyone would get up....but they just remain on the floor, silent and refusing to stand up. I want all the falling buildings, the bombs and the terrorist attacks to be just part of the special effects and no one will be hurt as a result. At the end of the movie the good guys win and it all ends and they live happily ever after. In the end, life isn't a script; it's the terrorist that dictates it.

Liya, 9th grade, Eilat

הייתי רוצה לדמיין שכל פעם שאני רואה חדשות ומבשרים על פיגוע שאירע ובאותו הזמן מראים ברקע את כל האנשים הצועקים, הבוכים ואלו המנסים במאמץ ובתקווה אולי להגיע ולמצוא אדם יקר לליבם קרוב משפחה, חבר או חברה או אפילו אדם זר שראו לפני שנייה. שכול אלו יהיו שחקנים על הסט שהבמאי עוד מעט יאמר "קאט" והם יוכלו לקום להפסקה ולהמשיך בחייהם אבל פשוט נשארים שרויים על הרצפה דוממים ומסרבים לקום. אני רוצה שכל הבניינים המתמוטטים, הפצצות, הפיגועים יהיו רק חלק מאפקט ואף אחד לא נפגע כתוצאה ממנו. ובסוף הסרט הטובים מנצחם והכול נגמר והם חיים באושר עד עצם היום הזה. בסופו של דבר החיים לא נכתבים על פי תסריט אבל הטרוריסטים מכתיבים לנו.

ליה, כיתה ט', אילת

كنت سأريد أن أتخيل أن كل مرة أشاهد فيها نشرة إخبارية ويعلنون بعملية إرهابية قد طرأت, وفي نفس الوقت يعرضون في الخلفية جميع الناس الصائحين والباكين والذين يحاولون ويبذلون جهدًا أملاً بإيجاد شخص عزيز من أقاربهم, أو صديق أو صديقة أو حتى شخص غريب قد لاحظوه قبل ثانية, أريد أن أتخيل أن جميعهم ممثلون سينمائيون وبعد قليل سيقول المخرج "كات", وسيتمكنون من النهوض في الاستراحة ومواصلة حياتهم. ولكنهم يبقون مستلقين على الأرض, جامدين ويرفضون النهوض. أريد أن أن جميع المباني المنهارة والقنابل والعمليات الإرهابية ستكون جزءًا من إنتاج سينمائي فقط ولا أحد سيصاب نتيجة منه. وفي نهاية الفيلم سينتصر الصالحون وكل شيء سينتهي وهم لا يزالون على قيد الحياة حتى يومنا هذا. وفي نهاية الأمر لا تسير الحياة حسب سيناريو ولكن الإرهابيين هم الذين يملون علينا سير الحياة.

www.israelikidsletterstoterrorists.com

I'll speak on behalf of all the people who think like me. We all ask for just one thing: Peace! And we can achieve this peace in several ways through goodwill and cooperation. I hope you'll understand, take it in and show some sensitivity.

Ana, 9th grade, Acre

אני אדבר בשם כל האנשים שאני חושבת שחושבים כמוני, כולנו מבקשים רק דבר אחד . . ואת השלום הזה אנחנו יכולים להשיג בכמה דרכים: רצון ושיתוף פעולה מקווה שתבין ותפנים ותראה טיפה רגישות ....

אנה, כיתה ט', עכו

إنني أتكلم باسم جميع الناس الذين أعتقد بأنهم سيعتقدون مثلي. نطلب كلنا شيئًا واحدًا فقط وهو السلام! ويمكننا أن نتوصل إلى هذا السلام ببعض الطرق منها الإرادة والتعاون. آمل بأنك ستدرك ذلك وستذوت ما تدركه وتُظهر الشيء القليل من الحساسية.

أنا, الصف التاسع, عكا

Do you know the word peace? Surely you do; you're fighting against it? Do you know how many people are working hard for this word? I just can't get how you can hate so much. I was raised to love people and to accept people who are different from me. And you're willing to throw away your life for unfounded hate? Who are you? You're not God, You have no right to take life away from people. Peace out?

Shailee, 9th grade, Eilat

מכיר את המילה שלום?
בטח שאתה מכיר את המילה הרי אתה נלחם בה.
האם אתה יודע כמה אנשים עובדים קשה בשביל המילה הזאת?
זה פשוט לא נקלט לי איך אפשר לשנוא ככה?
אותי גידולו בחינוך של לאהוב אנשים ולקבל אנשים ששונים ממך.
ואת כל החיים שלך אתה מוכן להשליך על שנאת חינם?!
מי אתה? אתה לא ה' אין לך זכות לקחת חיים
Peace out

שי-לי, כיתה ט', אילת

هل تعرف كلمة "سلام"؟
أكيد أنك تعرف, لأنك تحاربه.
هل تعرف إلى أي مدى يعمل الناس عملاً شاقًا من أجل هذه الكلمة؟
إنني لا أدرك كيف يمكن كره الناس إلى هذا الحد؟
لقد تربيت على محبة الناس وعلى قبول الناس الذين يختلفون عنك.
وأنت مستعد لتكرس حياتك كلها لكراهية لا مبرر لها؟!
من أنت؟ إنك ليس الله تعالى, ولا حق لك أن تسلب الحياة.
Peace out

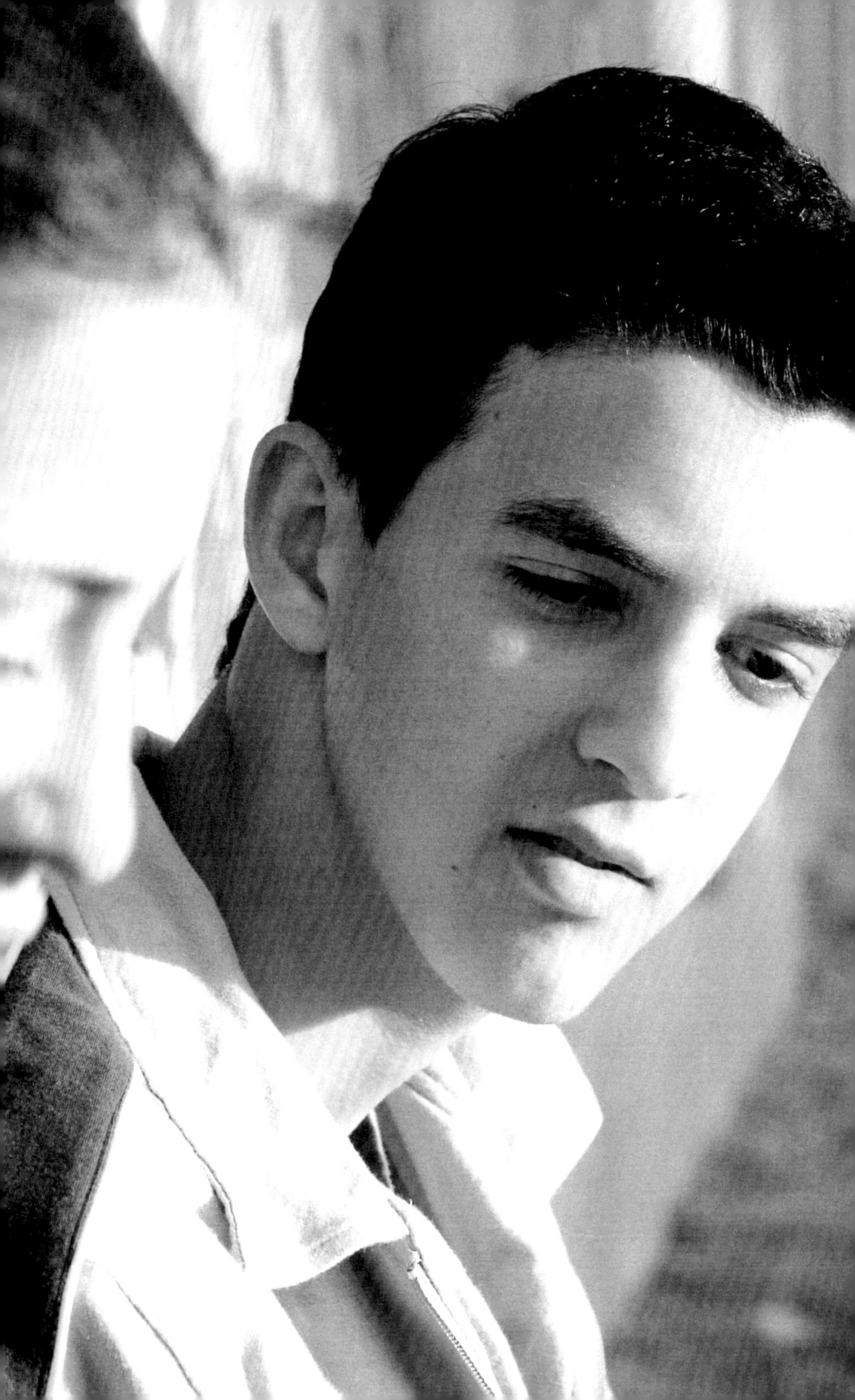

Believe me, there are better ways to achieve your goals. Take a moment and think about it. I'm sure that this isn't what you wanted to be when you were little. I'm sure that this is not what you prayed for. Just try to think for a moment what would have happened if things had turned out differently. You might understand that perhaps you're not on the right track. But to do so, I have to ask you to give up your position for a moment. I know it's hard, but try to see the other side for a moment, and see how you feel about thing.

Good bye,

Aviad, 11th grade, Beit She'an

תאמין לי, יש דרכים יותר טובות להשיג את המטרות שלך. קח רגע, תחשוב על זה, אני בטוח שזה לא מה שרצית להיות כשהיית קטן. אני בטוח שלא לזה ייחלת. פשוט תנסה לרגע לחשוב מה היה קורה אילו הדברים היו מסתדרים אחרת ואולי תבין שאתה לא פועל בדרך הנכונה. אבל בשביל זה אני מבקש ממך לוותר לרגע על העמדה שלך, אני יודע שזה קשה, אבל לרגע תנסה לראות את הצד השני, ותראה איך תרגיש....

שלום.

אביעד, כיתה י"א, בית שאן

صدقني, هناك طرق أفضل لتحقيق أهدافك. قف لحظة وفكر بذلك. إنني متأكد أن ما أنت عليه اليوم ليس ما رغبت به عندما كنت صغيرًا. إنني متأكد أنه ليس ذلك ما تمنيته. حاول لحظة أن تفكر بما كان سيحدث لو كانت الأمور تسير على مسلك آخر, وعندئذٍ لعلك تدرك أنك لا تعمل بالطريقة السليمة. غير أنني, أطلبك من أجل ذلك أن تتخلى ولو

How do you have the internal strength that drives you to do such terrible things? And then living with it, sleeping every night with that thought that never fades away? Don't you have a conscience?

Pupil, 11th grade, Eilat

איך יש לך את הכוח הפנימי, את הדבר הזה שמניע אותך לבצע דברים נוראים כאלה? ואחר כך עוד לחיות עם זה. לישון כל לילה עם המחשבה שלעולם לא תימוג. אין לך מצפון???

כיתה י"א, אילת

من أين لديك هذه القوة الداخلية التي تدفعك إلى تنفيذ أعمال فظيعة مثل هذه؟ ثم تعيش مع ذلك وتنام كل ليلة مع أفكار لا يمكن أن تتركك أليس لديك ضمير؟

الصف الحادي عشر, إيلات

Israeli Kids' Letters to Terrorists

Why can't you maybe live just like a normal person?! Get married, have a family, find a respectable livelihood, get old and eventually die. You could go to a support group in order to treat your problem, to regain your self-esteem.

Wishing you success,
Moshe, 9th grade, Ramle

למה אתה פשוט לא יכול לחיות חיים של בנאדם נורמאלי?! להתחתן להקים משפחה להתפרנס בכבוד, להזדקן ובסופו של יום למות. אתה יכול ללכת לקבוצת תמיכה, בכדי לטפל בבעיה שלך בכדי להחזיר לעצמך את ההערכה העצמית שאין לך.
מאחל לך בהצלחה,
משה, כיתה ט׳, רמלה

لماذا لا تستطيع أن تعيش حياة إنسان عادي!؟ أن تتزوج وتبني عائلة وتعيل نفسك وعائلتك بشكل محترم, وتشيخ, وفي نهاية المطاف ستموت. يمكنك الاشتراك بمجموعة دعم لمعالجة المشكلة التي تعاني منها ولتعيد لنفسك التقدير الذاتي الذي تنقصه.
أتمنى لك التوفيق,
موشيه, الصف التاسع, الرملة

If you have to express your anger, don't take it out on other people; especially innocent ones. Go to the gym ... hit the punching bag, find work or a hobby. Find a friend or a girlfriend to hang out with, just not anything that will hurt people. I hope you'll make the right decision.

Tzah, 9th grade, Ramle

אם אתה צריך לפרוק את הכעס שלך אל תעשה זאת על אנשים במיוחד לא חפים מפשע, לך לחדר כושר או משהו, תרביץ לשק אגרוף. תמצא משהו אחר שיעסיק אותך, תמצא עבודה או תחביב, תמצא חבר או חברה לבלות איתם, רק לא בדרך שתפגע באנשים. תחשוב על זה. אני מקווה שתעשה את ההחלטה הנכונה.

צח , כיתה ט׳, רמלה

إذا شعرت بالحاجة إلى أن تنفس غضبك, فلا تأخذ ناسًا هدفًا لذلك. وخاصة ليس الناس الأبرياء. إذهب إلى نادي اللياقة البدنية أو إلى مكان آخر مثله, واضرب كيس الملاكمة. جد لنفسك شيئًا آخر تهتم به. جد عملاً أو هواية. جد صديقًا أو صديقة تتسلى معهما. المهم هو ألا تصيب الناس. فكر بذلك. إنني آمل بأنك سوف تتخذ القرار السليم.

تساح, الصف التاسع, الرملة

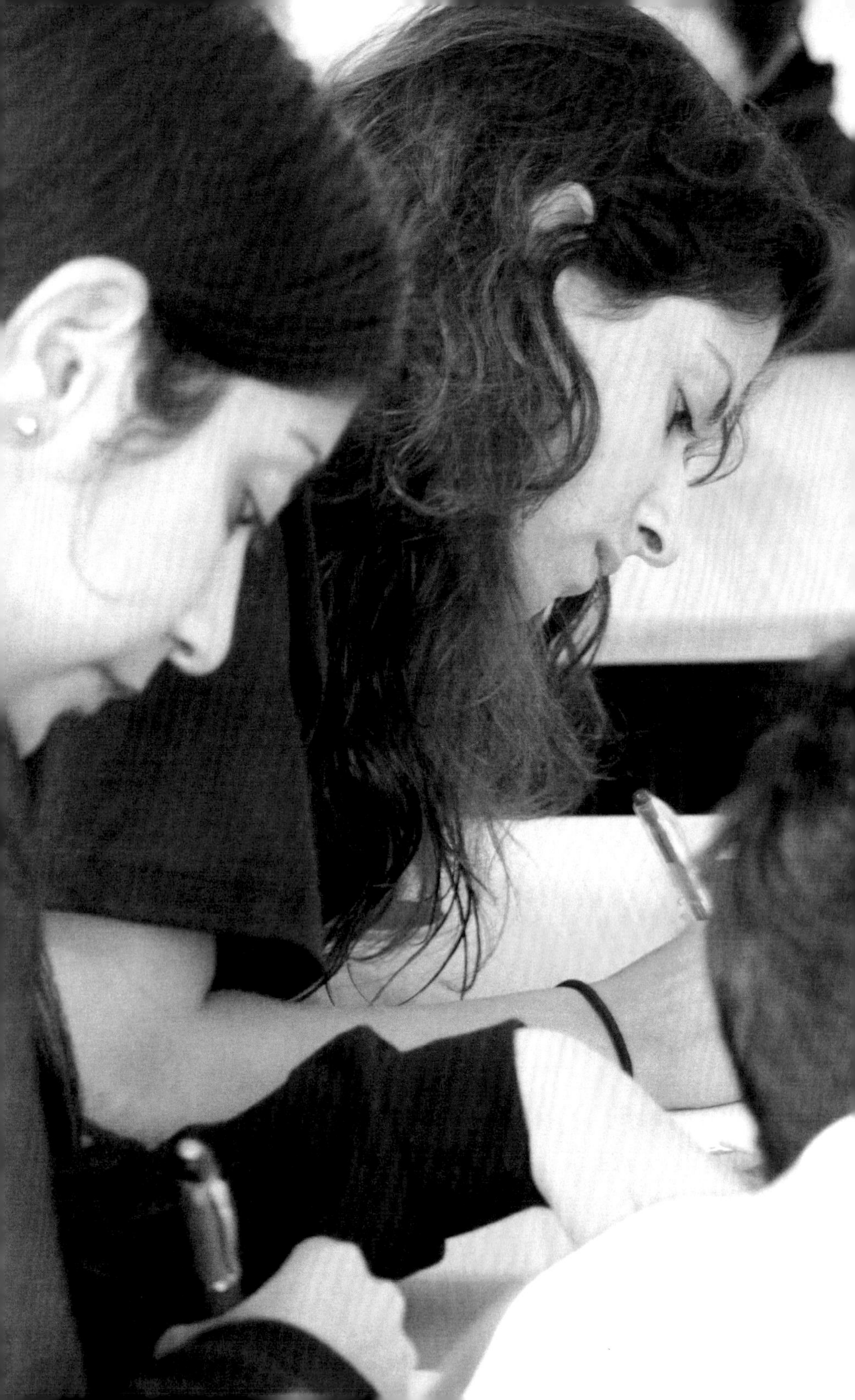

When people invest they usually have a good reason for doing so. Most people invest in assets or other positive things. Well, I don't find anything positive in terror so I don't see a reason to invest in terror. It's better for you to show more humaneness and compassion, than materialism and aggressiveness. Take this into consideration.

Nir, 11th grade, Ramle

אם אנשים משקיעים במשהו כנראה שיש להם סיבה טובה, לרוב אנשים משקיעים בנכסים או בדברים חיוביים. דבר ראשון, בטרור אני לא מוצא משהו חיובי וגם אני לא רואה סיבה להשקיע בטרור.
עדיף שתגלה יותר הומאניות, רגשיות מאשר חומריות וכוחניות.
קח את העניינים הנ"ל בחשבון ,

ניר, כיתה י"א, רמלה

إذا استثمر الناس بشيء ما فمن المؤكد أن لديهم مبرر جيد لذلك. غالباً ما يستثمر الناس بالممتلكات أو بالأشياء الإيجابية. أولاً, لا أجد أي وجه إيجابي بالإرهاب ,
ولا أجد أي سبب للاستثمار بالإرهاب.
من المفضل أن تُظهر أكثر إنسانية وعاطفية من المادية والعنف.
خذ ذلك بالحسبان.

نير, الصف الحادي عشر, الرملة

You should embrace life,
don't flush it down the toilet.

Amihay, 11th grade, Ramle

עמיחי, כיתה י"א, רמלה

من المستحسن أن تعانق الحياة ولا ترميها إلى بيت الماء وتسيلها إلى المجاري.
عاميحاي, الصف الحادي عشر, الرملة

www.israelikidsletterstoterrorists.com

I am a girl from Sderot, age 15 1/2, suffering from anxiety. I am being treated by psychologists, counselors and various therapists due to the Qassams, which are being shot into the Gaza Circumference settlements in Sderot. A very close person to me was killed by the first Qassam. This child was walking with his mother in the street when the Qassam suddenly fell, without any warning, without any sign. When I heard that he was killed I became traumatized and since then, I'm in a state of shock every time you launch the missiles at us.

Shelly, 10th grade, Sderot.

אני ילדה משדרות, בת 15 וחצי, נפגעת חרדה, מטופלת אצל פסיכולוגים, יועצים ומטפלים למיניהם עקב הקסאמים עקב ירי הקסאם לעבר ישובי עוטף עזה ושדרות. אדם קרוב מאוד אליי נהרג מהקסאם הראשון שהרג והיווה סכנה ממשית, באותו הזמן לא הייתה ההתרעה "צבע אדום" ובמקרה הלך אותו ילד שנהרג ואמו ברחוב כשלפתע נפל קסאם, ללא כל התרעה מוקדמת, ללא כל סימן לפני כן. כשנודע לי שהוא נהרג פשוט נכנסתי לטראומה ובכל פעם, מאז שהוא נהרג, אני נתקפת הלם כשיש שיגור רקטות לעברנו.

שלי, כיתה י', שדרות

إنني فتاة من سديروت, عمري 15 سنة والنصف, أعاني من الهلع, وتتم معالجتي على أيدي علماء النفس والمستشارين وأنواع مختلفة من المعالجين. وذلك بسبب إطلاق صواريخ القسام باتجاه البلدات المتاخمة لقطاع غزة وسديروت.
وقد قتل شخص قريب مني جدًا من أول صواريخ القسام الذي سبب القتل وشكل خطرًا فعليًا. وفي نفس الوقت لم يوجد إنذار "اللون الأحمر", وعلى طريق الصدفة مشى ذلك الولد الذي قتل في الشارع مع أمه عندما سقط صاروخ قسام فجأة, دون أي إنذار مبكر. عندما علمت بأنه قد قتل أصبت بالصدمة النفسية. وكل مرة. منذ قتله, عندما يحدث إطلاق الصواريخ باتجاهنا, أصاب بصدمة.

Once upon a time, life was better. Today, it's best to dream about distant places, perhaps Mars, where there's no air to breathe, but at least there are no terrorists either!

Sandra, 12th grade, Ramle

פעם, החיים היו טובים יותר היום כבר עדיף לשקוע בחלומות על מקומות רחוקים אולי על המאדים, שם לפחות אין אוויר לנשימה אבל לפחות שם אין טרוריסטים!

סנדרה, כיתה י"ב, רמלה

في الماضي, كانت الحياة أحسن ما هي عليه اليوم. أما اليوم, فمن المفضل أن نغرق بالأحلام حول أماكن نائية, من الممكن حول المريخ. لا يوجد هناك هواء للتنفس ولكن, على الأقل, لا يوجد هناك إرهابيون!

ساندرا, الصف الثاني عشر, الرملة

Seven years of Qassam missiles fired at us every day. Believe me when I tell you we've fed up and can't take it anymore. Every Qassam that falls is met with growing apathy. Sadly we have just gotten used to living in this situation. Just try to understand us. I don't know if you'll really pay attention to this letter or whether it'll just motivate you to continue firing the Qassams. It's your decision. I just wanted to share with you a small part of what I am feeling.
From me, a victim of your terrorism.

Avia, 9th grade, Sderot

7 שנים של קסאמים מדי יום, תאמין לי שזה כבר נמאס ואין לנו כוח.
כל קסאם שנופל זה כבר – 'יאללה נפל עוד קסאם' . פשוט התרגלנו לחיות במצב הזה, לצערנו.
רק תנסה להבין אותנו. אני לא יודעת אם באמת תתייחס למכתב הזה או שזה פשוט ייתן לך עוד מוטיבציה להמשיך.
זו החלטה שלך. רק שיתפתי אותך בחלק קטן ממה שאני מרגישה.

ממני,
נפגעת מהטרור שלך.

אביה, כיתה ט', שדרות

سبع سنوات من صواريخ القسام التي تطلق يوميًا. صدقني أننا مللنا من هذه الأوضاع ونفذت قوانا.
رد فعلنا على كل صاروخ قسام الذي يسقط – "يا الله قد سقط صاروخ قسام آخر". تعودنا إلى العيش بهذه الحالة, لأسفنا الشديد.
حاول أن تفهمنا فقط. لا أعرف إذا انتبهت حقًا إلى هذا المكتوب أو أنه سيكون بالنسبة إليك دافعًا للاستمرار بأعمالك.
هذا هو قرارك. إنني شاركتك فقط بالشيء القليل مما أشعر به.
مني,

I'm only asking God to help you because a person who is doing such horrible things is mentally ill and needs treatment. A normal, sane person would never do such things. I really hope that God will help you and that as the end of your days comes upon you, you will not regret what you did.

Caroline, 11th grade, Ramle

אני רק מבקשת שאלוהים יעזור לך כי אדם שעושה מעשים כאלה הוא חולה נפש ואדם שצריך טיפול כי מעשים כאלה, אדם נורמאלי, שפוי בדעתו בחיים לא היה עושה.
אני באמת מקווה שאלוהים יעזור לך ושבסוף ימייך לא תתחרט על מה שעשית אבל לומר את האמת אני די בטוחה שאתה אף פעם לא תתחרט

קרולין, כיתה י"א, רמלה

إنني أطلب فقط أن يساعدك الله, لأن إنسانًا يقوم بأعمال مثل هذه هو مريض عقليًّا ويحتاج إلى علاج. لأن الإنسان العادي السليم العقل لم يمكن أنه يقوم بهذه الأعمال أبدًا.
أرجو أن يساعدك الله وأنك, في نهاية عمرك سوف تندم على ما قمت به. ولكنه, إذا قلت الحق, فإنني متأكدة تمامًا أنك لا تندم أبدًا.
كارولين, الصف الحادي عشر, الرملة

If you want to get back (conquered) territories, just announce a fair war so that our side, too, will be able to fight, and it would be possible to say who lost and who won. It also wouldn't last such a long time and there would be less killing.

Ella, 9th grade, Sderot.

אם אתה רוצה להחזיר (לכבוש) שטחים, פשוט תכריז על מלחמה הוגנת כדי שגם הצד שלנו יוכל להלחם, וניתן יהיה לקבוע מי המנצח ומי המפסיד, וגם כדי שלא ימשך הרבה זמן ויהיו פחות הרוגים.

אלה, כיתה ט', שדרות

إذا أردت استرداد (احتلال) الأراضي, فأعلن فقط عن حرب نزيهة ليتمكن طرفنا من المحاربة أيضاً, وسيكون من الممكن تحديد الفائز والخاسر, وكذلك لئلا تستمر الحرب مدة طويلة وسيقل عدد القتلى.

إيلا, الصف التاسع, سديروت

What's in it for you? Try to also understand the other side. I could go right now and launch an attack upon you, but I'm not doing it, right? Because I know this is not the way to solve problems. I bet you know it too! Now think: Do you really want to carry out a terrorist attack? Well, it's up to you...

Gal, 9th grade, Acre

תנסה להבין גם את הצד השני.. גם אני עכשיו יכולה לקום ולעשות פיגוע, אבל אני לא עושה את זה נכון?? כי אני יודעת שזאת לא הדרך לפתור בעיות. ואני בטוחה שגם אתה יודע!...
עכשיו תקרא ותחשוב.. אתה באמת רוצה לעשות פיגוע? טוב זאת כבר החלטה שלך....

גל, כיתה ט', עכו

حاول أن تفهم الطرف الآخر أيضًا. إنني أستطيع أن أنفذ عملية إرهابية الآن أيضًا, ولكنني لا أعمل ذلك. أليس كذلك؟؟ ذلك لأنني أعلم أن هذه ليست الطريقة الصحيحة لحل المشاكل, وأنا إمتأكدة أنك تعلم ذلك أيضًا ...
... والآن, اقرأ كلامي وفكر.. هل تريد حقًا أن تنفذ عملية إرهابية؟ حسنًا, هذا هو قرارك

غال, الصف التاسع, عكا

Before reading this letter, I want to tell you to read it as if I'm your closest friend. Just for a minute, think on your own: Is it "worth" it? Just for a minute, open the Koran and read it, study it. Don't look at the interpretations and statements of people, just read and make up your own mind. When you finish, find out where it says that you should kill people. Check it out. Is it written there, or were you told different interpretations and stories about the Koran?

Pupil, 9th grade, Acre

לפני שאתה קורא מכתב זה, אני רוצה שתקרא אותו, כאילו אני חבר קרוב שלך.
מאוד קרוב. רק לרגע, וחשוב עם עצמך: האם זה "שווה את זה"? פתח לרגע את הקוראן וקרא אותו, למד אותו. אל תסתכל בפירושים והיגדים של אנשים, פשוט קרא והבע את דעתך שלך. שתסיים, בדוק היכן כתוב שעליך להרוג בני אדם. בדוק, האם זה כתוב שם, או שסתם סיפרו לי פירושים שונים וסיפורים שונים של הקוראן?

חניך, כיתה ט', עכו

قبل أن تقرأ هذا المكتوب أريد أن تقرأه كأنني صديقك المخلص. مخلص للغاية. للحظة فقط. وفكر في قلبك: هل هذا "يستحق ذلك"؟
إفتح لحظة القرآن الكريم واقرأه, ادرسه. لا تنظر إلى التفاسير وأقوال الناس. إقرأ فقط وعبر عن رأيك. عندما تنتهي من ذلك, افحص أين يذكر أنه يجب عليك أن تقتل الناس. إفحص, هل ذلك مكتوب هناك أو حكوا لك تفاسير مختلفة وحكايات مختلفة عن القرآن؟
طالب, الصف التاسع, عكا

You crossed the line a bit, don't you think? I think that if we stop this cycle of hurt and revenge, we would be introducing something that has never existed before, a basis for mutual existence, the accomplishment of which perhaps the grandchildren of our grandchildren will live to enjoy. I hope I have managed to give you my opinion, and if I succeeded in changing anything, even one little thing in the way you think, then this letter has probably fulfilled its role in the world and it was worth the time invested in writing it. I wish you as long and as enjoyable a life as possible.

Mor, 10th grade, Ramle

אני חושבת שאם נעצור את המעגל הזה, של הפגיעה והנקמה, ננהיג פה משהו חדש, שעוד לא היה, בסיס לקיום הדדי שאולי נכדי נכדינו יוכלו ליהנות משלמותו.
אני מקווה שהצלחתי להקנות לך את דעתי, ואם הצלחתי לשנות דבר, ולו דבר אחד בדרכי חשיבתך- אז כנראה שהמכתב הזה קיים את ייעודו בעולם ושהיה שווה להקדיש זמן לכתיבתו.
המשך חיים מהנים וארוכים (עד כמה שאפשר) , מור.

מור, כיתה י', רמלה

إنني أعتقد أنه إذا أوقفنا هذه الدائرة, دائرة الإصابات والانتقام, فسنبني هنا شيء جديد, لم يكن مثله في الماضي, ويشكل قاعدة للتعايش ولعل أحفاد أحفادنا سيتمكنون من التمتع بسلامته.
آمل أنني نجحت بشرح رأيي لك. وإذا نجحت بتغيير شيء ما عندك, ولو شيء واحد في طرق تفكيرك – فيبدو أن هذا المكتوب حقق غايته في العالم وكان من اللائق أن أكرس الوقت لكتابته.
أتمنى لكلنا مواصلة الحياة الممتعة والطويلة (إلى أقصى حد يمكن). مور.

مور, الصف العاشر, الرملة

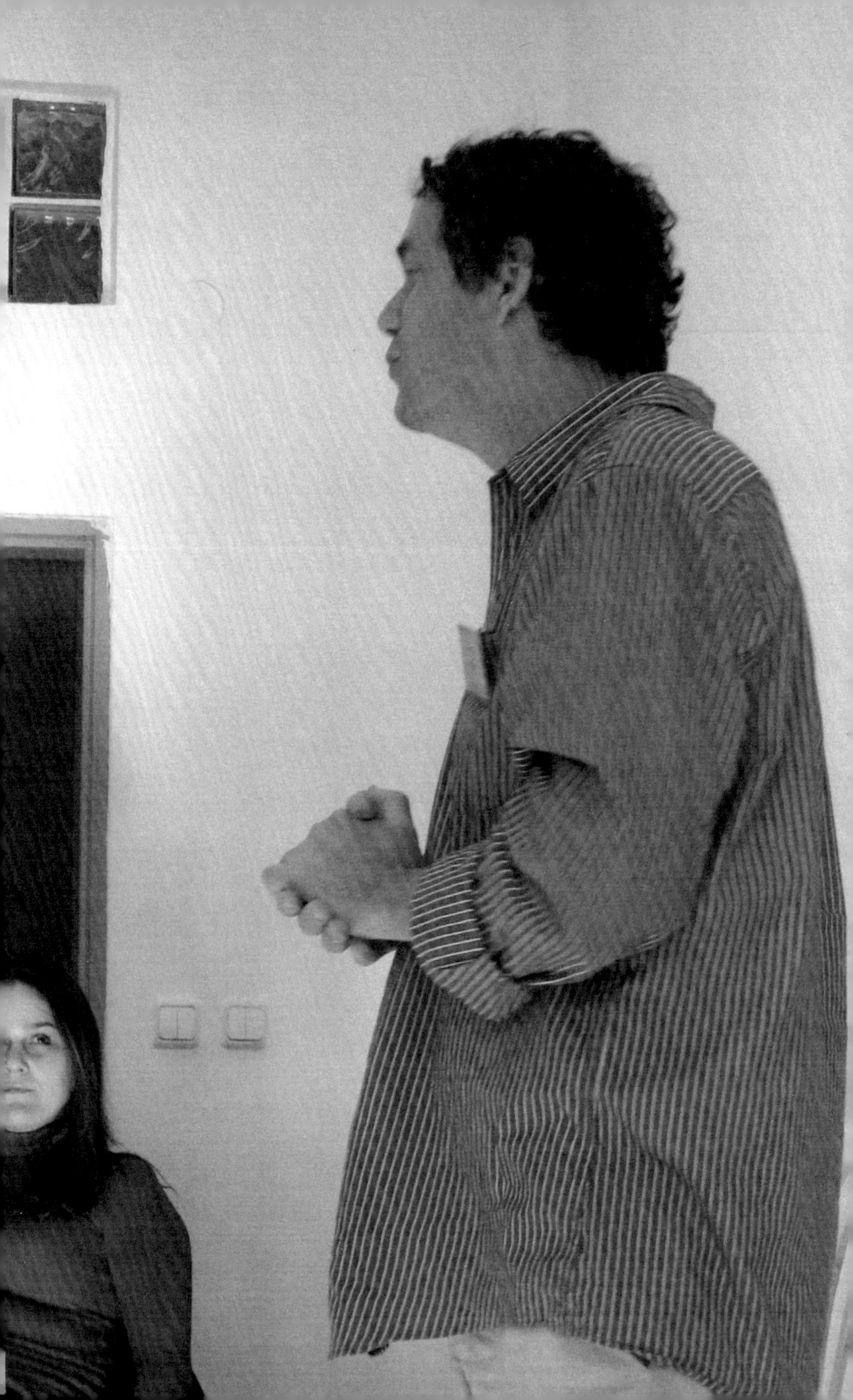

Do something with your life,
and if you have a problem,
talk to someone.

Tomer, 11th grade, Ramle

תעשה משהו עם החיים שלך ואם יש לך
בעיה, תדבר עם מישהו.
תומר, כיתה י"א, רמלה

إعمل شيئًا ما مع حياتك, وإذا كانت لديك أية مشكلة
فتحدث مع شخص ما.
تومر, الصف الحادي عشر, الرملة

www.israelikidsletterstoterrorists.com

I'm a 16-year-old Christian. Everyone dreams of world peace, but I dream only of quiet. To hear that soldiers have died is painful, to hear that Arabs have died is painful and to hear that people on the street have died is painful, regardless of their religion.

Bisan, 10th grade, Ramle

אני בת 16, נוצרייה. כולם חולמים על שלום בעולם, ואני חולמת רק על שקט.
לשמוע שמתו חיילים זה כואב ולשמוע שמתו ערבים זה כואב ולשמוע שמתו אנשים ברחוב זה כואב... ולא משנה לאיזה דת הם שייכים.

ביסאן , כיתה י', רמלה

عمري 16 سنة وأنا مسيحية. الكل يحلم بحلول السلام في العالم, وأنا أحلم بالهدوء فقط.
من المؤلم أن نسمع بقتل الجنود ومن المؤلم أن نسمع بقتل العرب ومن المؤلم أن نسمع بأن ناسًا قد ماتوا في الشارع .... ولا يهم ما هي داينتهم.

بيسان, الصف العاشر, الرملة

Don't you understand that we've had it, all of us (the Jews and I guess many of the Arabs, too), with this ongoing war? We can't take it anymore. I can't take it anymore. Instead of living a peaceful life like other children my age all over the world, I have to cope with the terrorism that you are constantly inflicting upon us. Just stop it! You're killing people; we're killing people. Even if according to the "experts" one side won, tell me, what was won? Victory is not conquering a lot of territory. Victory is reaching a compromise that fits all, without all the killing.

Lydia, 10th grade, Sderot

אתם לא מבינים שנמאס לנו, לכולנו (גם ליהודים, ואני מניחה שגם לרבים מהערבים), מכל המלחמה המתמשכת הזאת? אין לנו כוח יותר. אין לי כוח יותר. במקום לחיות חיים שקטים ושלווים כמו ילדים בני גילי ברחבי העולם, אני צריכה להתמודד, גם עם הטרור המתמשך שאתם מנחיתים עלינו. פשוט די. זה כל מה שאני מבקשת ממך, די.
אתם הורגים אנשים, אנחנו הורגים אנשים, וגם אם עפ"י ה'מומחים' צד כלשהו ניצח, תסביר לי, במה הוא ניצח כביכול? בזה שהוא איבד עשרות אנשים? זה ניצחון? ניצחון זה לא לכבוש הרבה שטחים. ניצחון זה להגיע לפשרה שמתאימה לכולם, בלי כל ההרג הזה מסביב.

לידיה, כיתה י', שדרות

ألا تفهمون أننا مللنا كلنا (اليهود, وأفترض أن الكثير من العرب أيضًا) بهذه الحرب المستمرة؟ لم تبق قوة لدينا. لم تبق قوة لدي. بدلاً من أن نعيش حياة هادئة مثل فتيان وفتيات في عمري في جميع أنحاء العالم, يجب علي أن أواجه الإرهاب المستمر الذي تضربوننا به. كفاية. كل ما أطلب منك هو: كفاية.
إنكم تقتلون ناسًا. نحن نقتل ناسًا. وحتى إذا اعتقد "الخبراء" أن أحد الطرفين انتصر, فاشرح لي من فضلك ما هو انتصاره فعلاً؟ هل انتصر عندما فقد عشرات من الناس؟ هل هذا ما يسمى انتصارًا؟ ليس الانتصار احتلال الكثير من الأراضي. الانتصار هو التوصل إلى التسوية , إلى حل الوسط الذي يلائم كلنا, دون كل هذا القتل الذي يحيطنا.

ليديا, الصف العاشر, سديروت

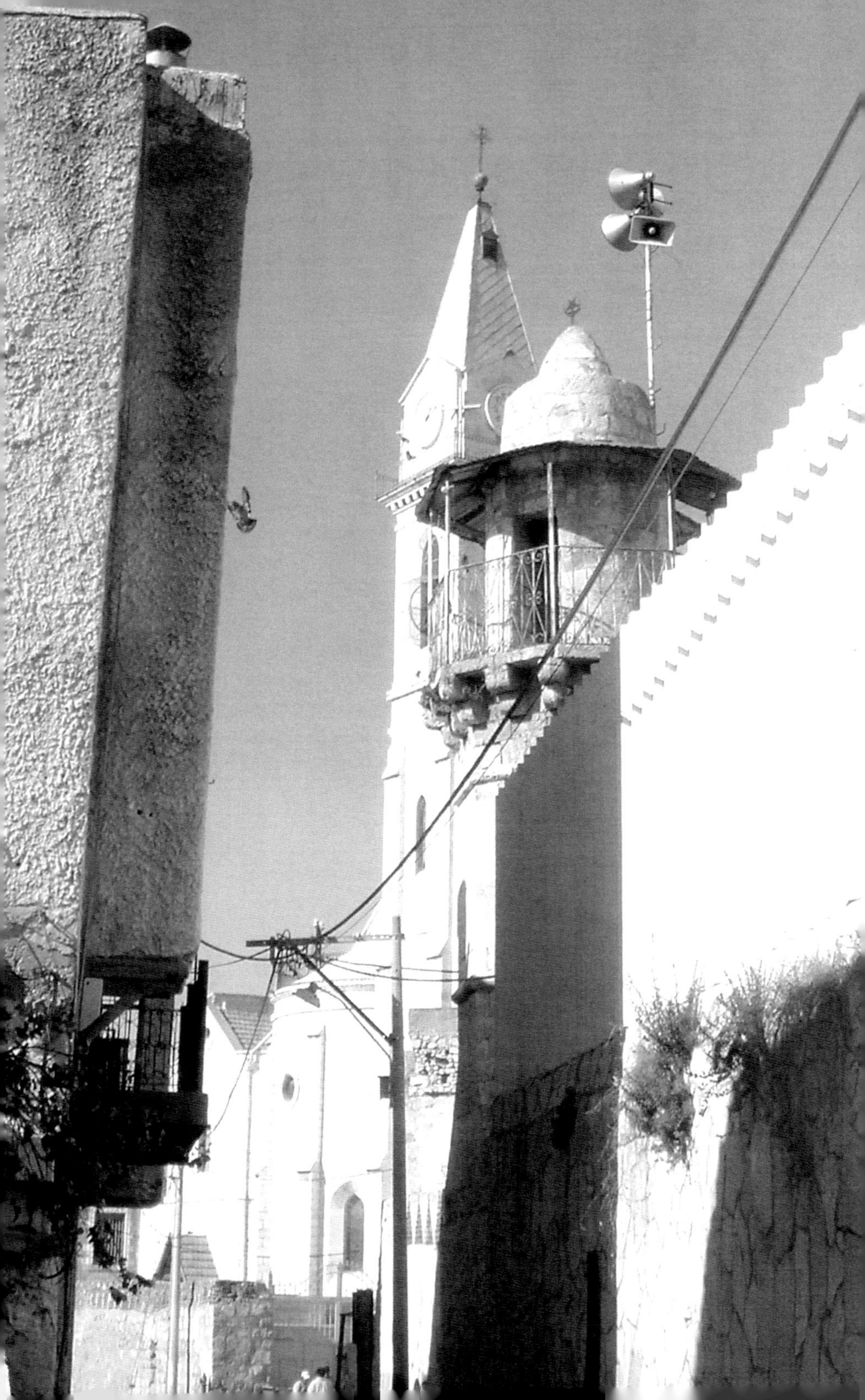

Want to give up terrorism?   We hereby present an offer that you can't refuse. If you stop your hostile acts against the organizations or the countries you attack, we offer you a great substitute: the association of "ex-terrorists." Come today to one of our branches, bring in your Kalashnikov and get a dummy gun--friendly to the environment. Get the perfect substitute: the struggle for the quality of the environment. Why get busy with dirty matters when you can be busy with cleaning? Instead of being busy separating 3.8 mm from 9 mm guns, please come and separate glass from plastic.

Yehiel, 10th grade, Ramle

? רוצים להתנתק מהטרוריזם
הרינו מציגים בפניך הצעה שלא תוכל לסרב לה, אם תפסיק עם פעולות האיבה כנגד הארגונים או המדינות שאתה מבצע נגדם פעולות אלה נציע לך תחליף נהדר:
עמותת "טרוריסטים לשעבר" מציעה לך להגיד לטרור-שלום. אז בוא גם אתה להיגמל מהטרוריזם –ללא כאבים,וללא ייסורי מצפון. הצטרף עוד היום לעשרות הטרוריסטים שכבר אומרים:טרוריסטים נמאסנו!
הגיעו עוד היום לאחד מהסניפים שלנו,החזירו את הקלצ'ניקוב וקבלו רובה-דמה ידידותי לסביבה עם סט חזיזים מהודר-מתנה.
קבלו את התחליף המושלם-המאבק למען איכות הסביבה.
למה לכם להתעסק בעסקים המלוכלכים שאתם יכולים להתעסק בניקיון?
במקום להתעסק בהפרדה בין קליבר 3.8 מ"מ לבין קליבר 9 מ"מ, בואו להתעסק בהפרדה בין זכוכית ופלסטיק.

יחיאל כיתה י', רמלה

هل تريدون الانفصال عن الإرهاب؟
نعرض عليك نصيحة لا يمكنكم رفضها. إذا توقفت عن ممارسة الأعمال العدوانية ضد المنظمات أو الدول التي تقوم بهذه الأعمال ضدها, فسنعرض عليك بديلاً رائعًا:
تعرض عليك جمعية "إرهابيون سابقاً" أن تودع الإرهاب. تعال أنت أيضًا وانفطم عن الإرهاب – دون آلام ودون تأنيب الضمير. إنضم حتى اليوم إلى الإرهابيين الذين يقولون: مَلّ بنا الناس, أيها الإرهابيون!
صلوا حتى اليوم إلى أحد فروعنا, أعيدوا الكلاشنيكوف واستلموا بندقية لعبة ودية للبيئة مع مجموعة من القنابل الصوتية الرائعة هدية لكم.
إستلموا البديل المثالي – الكفاح من أجل حماية البيئة.
لماذا تمارسون الأشياء الوسخة عندما يمكنكم ممارسة التنظيف؟
بدلاً من ممارسة التصنيف ما بين معيار 3.8 ملم ومعيار 9 ملم, تعالوا مارسوا التصنيف ما بين الزجاج والبلاستيك.

يحيئل, الصف العاشر, الرملة

When God gave out wisdom to the whole world, you just weren't there! I have some advice for you: instead of hurting people and destroying houses, there's a much simpler and more effective way for all of us… you can meet with the people who "wronged you", fix your problems and everything will be all right, because, after all, you're human, and as far as I know, humans understand each other and can forgive one another. Please, terrorist, do as I say. You won't be sorry.

Marian, 9th grade, Ramle

וגם כשאלוהים חילק שכל לעולם כולו אתה פשוט לא הייתה נוכח.
יש לי עצה בשבילך-במקום ללכת ולפגוע באנשים אחרים ולהרוס בתים יש דרך יותר פשוטה ויותר יעלה לכולנו.... אתה יכול להיפגש עם האנשים "שמעוללים לך רע" לסדר את כל הבעיות והכל יהיה בסדר כי בסך הכל אתם תישארו בני אדם וכשידוע לי בני אדם מבינים זה את זה ויכולים לסלוח אחד לשני כי עצתו של אלוהים כי לאהוב ולסלוח אחד לשני תמיד.
בבקשה טרוריסט עשה כדברי אתה לא תצטער .

מריאן, כיתה ט', רמלה

.عندما وزع الله تعالى العقل على العالم كله, فأنت لم تحضر
لدي نصيحة أعرضها عليك: بدلاً من إصابة الناس وتدمير البيوت هناك طريقة أكثر بساطة وأكثر نجاعة بالنسبة لجميعنا ... يمكنك أن تلتقي بالناس الذين "يسيئون لك" وتسوي معهم المشاكل كلها والكل سيكون على أحسن ما يرام, في نهاية الأمر ستبقون ناسًا, وكما أعرف فان الناس يتفاهمون مع البعض ويمكن أن يتسامحوا البعض. وذلك لأن نصيحة الله تعالى هي أن تسود المحبة والتسامح بين الناس دائمًا.
من فضلك, يا إرهابي, تصرف كما أعرض عليك ولن تندم.

ماريان, الصف العاشر, الرملة

Israeli Kids' Letters to Terrorists

It's true that talks cannot always solve all the problems we're facing today, but terror also doesn't achieve that goal. Try, just a little, to distance yourself from the world of terrorism, from violent solutions and the miserable life you chose for yourself... and for others. Try to work together with the world to really show that your cause is humane so that your views can be understood. Perhaps this way you'll achieve, at last, your goals, which are, naturally, not to kill innocent people and create a world of terror.

Eliana, 11th grade, Ramle

נכון, דיבור לא תמיד מביא לפתרון לכל הבעיות שניצבות מולנו כיום, אך הטרור גם אינו משיג את המטרה. נסו, רק לקצת להתרחק מעולם הטרור, מהפתרונות האלימים ומהחיים האומללים שהצבתם לעצמכם.. וגם לאחרים. נסו לעבוד יחד עם העולם כדי באמת להראות לו כי סיבותיכם הינן אנושיות, וכי את דעותיכן ניתן להבין. אולי כך, סוף סוף, תשיגו את מטרותיכם שכמובן אינן להרוג אנשים חפים מפשע וליצור עולם של טרור.

אליאנה, כיתה: י"א, רמלה

صحيح. إن الحوار لا يؤدي دائمًا إلى حل جميع القضايا التي تواجهنا في الوقت الحاضر. ولكن الإرهاب هو أيضًا لا يحقق الهدف. حاولوا أن تبتعدوا عن عالم الإرهاب, بعض الشيء, عن الحلول العنيفة والحياة البائسة التي حددتم لأنفسكم, وكذلك لغيركم. حاولوا أن تتعاونوا مع العالم لتثبتوا له بأن الأسباب التي تدفعكم هي أسباب إنسانية, وأن يمكن فهم آرائكم. لعلكم بهذه الطريقة ستحققون, في نهاية الأمر, أهدافكم التي هي, في طبيعة الحال, ليست قتل الأبرياء وخلق عالم من الإرهاب.

إليانا, الصف الحادي عشر, الرملة

Aren't you afraid of dying? I am. Death is the most frightening thing for me. If you don't value life, then you don't value anything else, that's for sure. You live just once. You probably don't understand the value of life, of living and experiencing, and doing the best with your life.

Shoval, 11th grade, Dimona

איך אתה לא מפחד למות?! מוות זה הדבר הכי מפחיד עבורי. אם אין לך ערך לחיים אין לך ערך לשום דבר אחר, זה בטוח.
חיים רק פעם אחת, אתה כנראה לא מבין את הערך של החיים, של לחיות ולחוות ולעשות את הטוב ביותר בחייך.

שובל, כיתה י"א, דימונה.

كيف لا تخاف من الموت؟! الموت, بالنسبة لي هو أشد شيء هلعًا. إذا لم تقدّر الحياة, فلا تقدّر أي شيء آخر, بالتأكيد.
نحن نعيش مرة واحدة فقط. فيما يبدو لا تدرك قيمة الحياة, ولا تدرك ما معنى العيش والتجرب وعمل الخير في حياتك.

شوفال, الصف الحادي عشر, ديمونا

Violence hasn't gotten us anywhere, at least not closer to peace, which is something I believe that we both want. Eventually, we all want some quiet. Why don't we try a little harder?

Tzlil, 11th grade, Dimona

באופן אלים לא הגענו ולא נגיע לשומקום, לפחות לא לאזור של שלום, דבר שאני מאמינה ששנינו רוצים.
בסופו של דבר, כולנו רוצים קצת שקט. למה שלא נשתדל קצת יותר בשביל שהוא יגיע?

צליל, כיתה י"א, דימונה

بالعنف لم نصل ولن نصل إلى أي مكان, ليس إلى منطقة سلمية, على الأقل. وذلك أمر أعتقد أن كلينا نريده. وفي نهاية الأمر, كلنا نريد بعض الهدوء. فلماذا لم نبذل المزيد من الجهود من أجل وصوله؟

تسليل, الصف الحادي عشر, ديمونة

Do you really believe you're going to have 72 virgins? Even if it were true, do you really think they'd want to be with a murderer?

Pupil, 9th grade, Dimona

אתה באמת מאמין שיהיו לך 72 בתולות?
וגם אם כן, אתה באמת חושב שהן ירצו להיות עם רוצח?

חניכה, כיתה ט', דימונה.

هل أنت تعتقد أن تكون لك 72 عذراء (حورية)؟
وإن صح ذلك, فهل تعتقد حقًا أنهن يردن معاشرة القاتل؟

طالبة, الصف التاسع, ديمونا

Israeli Kids' Letters to Terrorists

Don't think that I hate you. You're willing to sacrifice your life for your goals (though they're not ethical), and you're willing to fight for your nation (even if it's not formally defined as a state) in order to establish a state. Actually, you are sacrificing your life for something that may happen. That's nice. But, on the other hand, think about what you are doing. You can either blow yourself up and take people with you who did nothing to you, or you can stand on your principles in a different way, for the benefit of all.

Pupil, 10th grade, Dimona

אל תחשוב שאני שונא אותך, אתה מוכן להקריב את החיים שלך בשביל המטרות שלך (למרות שזה לא אתי), אתה מוכן להילחם בשביל עם, אפילו לא מדינה מוגדרת רשמית) כדי להקים מדינה.
בעצם, אתה מקריב את החיים שלך בשביל משהו שאולי יקום, זה כבר יפה אבל מצד שני תחשוב על מה שאתה עושה. אתה יכול להתפוצץ ולקחת איתך אנשים שממילא לא עשו לך כלום, או לעמוד על העקרונות שלך בדרך אחרת שתטיב עם כולם.

חניך, כיתה י', דימונה.

لا تعتقد بأنني أكرهك. أنت مستعد أن تضحي بحياتك في سبيل تحقيق أهدافك (رغم أن ذلك غير أخلاقي). أنت مستعد أن تكافح من أجل شعب (وحتى ليس من أجل دولة يعترف بها رسميًا) بهدف إقامة دولة.
وبالفعل, أنت تضحي بحياتك من أجل شيء يمكن أن يقوم. وذلك بحد ذاته, جدير بالتقدير ولكن, من جهة أخرى, فكر بما تعمله. من الممكن أن تنفجر وتأخذ معك ناسًا لم يسيئوا بك, أو بدلا من ذلك, يمكن أن تدافع عن مبادئك بطريقة أخرى تحسن للجميع.

طالب, الصف العاشر, ديمونا

You're frightened! What are you running away from? From whom are you trying to escape? You could have been a good man... You filled your life with emptiness ... Pity ...

Pupil, 9th grade, Dimona

אתה מפחד! ממה אתה בורח? ממי אתה מנסה לברוח?
היית יכול להיות אדם טוב...
מילאת את החיים שלך ריקנות...

חניכה, כיתה ט', דימונה.

أنت تخاف! مما تهرب؟ ممن تحاول الهروب؟
... كان من الممكن أن تكون إنسانًا طيب القلب
... لقد ملأت حياتك خواء

طالبة, الصف التاسع, ديمونا

I believe that a good person is someone who doesn't hurt others and tries to resolve his own problems without involving others. I know that you could fit this definition and be an amazing person in the future... Just forget the past, focus on the future, try to do your best to improve and always remember that you can do it.
There's always hope.

Nirvana, 10th grade, Ramle

אני מאמינה שאדם טוב הוא אדם שלא פוגע באחר ומנסה לסדר את הבעיות שלו בכוחות עצמו בלי לערב אחרים ואני יודעת שאתה יכול להתאים להגדרה הזאת ובעתיד להיות אחד האנשים המדהימים.... פשוט תשכח את העבר ותתמקד בעתיד ותנסה לעשות ככל יכולתך כדי לשפר אותו ותמיד תזכור שאתה מסוגל ותמיד יש תקווה תמיד אבל תמיד ....

נירוונה, כיתה י', רמלה

إنني أعتقد بأن الإنسان الطيب هو إنسان لا يمس أحدًا ويحاول تسوية أموره بنفسه دون توريط الآخرين. إنني أعرف أنه من الممكن أن تلائم هذا التعريف وستكون في المستقبل أحد الناس المدهشين ... إنسَ الماضي وتركز على المستقبل وحاول أن تعمل كل ما بوسعك لتحسين الأوضاع المستقبلية, وتذكر دائمًا أنك قادر على ذلك ودائمًا هناك أمل. دائمًا ...

نيرفانا, الصف العاشر, ديمونا

Isn't it possible for both sides to stop and to start a new way of communicating between our two worlds so we can live together? All it takes is to open a new page.

Ma'ayan, 10th grade, Eilat

אפשר פשוט ששני הצדדים יפסיקו וכך נתחיל דרך חדשה בין שני עולמותינו
ונוכל לחיות ביחד.
לזכור שרק צריך לפתוח דף חדש

מעין, אילת

من الممكن, ببساطة, أن الطرفين سيتوقفان عن أعمالهما, وهكذا نسير في طريق جديد بين عالمينا ويمكننا التعايش مع البعض.
يجب أن ننتبه إلى أنه يجب علينا فتح صفحة جديدة فقط.

ماعيان, إيلات

Bro, let's live in peace. You're frightening me! Right now you're not letting me go by bus, you don't let me walk in the street, I'm afraid that one of your brothers will shoot me or blow himself up while he's standing next to me, or that your car will explode in my street. Let's chill out, both of us, and sit together over a cup of coffee. I very much hope to see us both sitting over a knafe (sweet cake) real soon. Thank you and good bye.

Sahar, 12th grade, Beit She'an

אח שלי, בוא נחייה בשלום. אתה מפחיד אותי, כרגע אתה לא נותן לי לעלות לאוטובוס, לא נותן לי ללכת ברחוב, אני מפחד שאחד האחים שלך לא יירה בי או יתפוצץ עליי, או שהרכב שלך יתפוצץ ברחוב שלי. בוא נירגע שנינו ונשב ביחד על כוס קפה. אני מקווה מאוד שלקחת את הדברים לתשומת לבך מאוד מקווה לראות את שנינו יושבים ביחד על כנאפה בקרוב.
תודה רבה לך ולהתראות.

סהר, כיתה י"ב, בית שאן

يا أخي, تعال نعش بسلام. أنت تخيفني. لا تدعني الآن أركب الباص, ولا تدعني أمشي في الشارع. إنني أخاف أن أحد إخوانك يطلق علي النار أو ينفجر بقربي, أو أن تنفجر سيارتك في الشارع الذي أسكن فيه. تعال نهدأ كلانا ونقعد معًا ونشرب القهوة. إنني آمل جدًا أن تنتبه إلى كلامي غاية الانتباه, وآمل أن نقعد معًا قريبًا ونأكل الكنافة. شكرًا لك وإلى اللقاء.

ساهار, الصف الثاني عشر, بيت شآن

Say, that 72 virgin thing? I heard some things got mixed up...they're no longer virgins and they are 72 years old!

Udi, 11th grade, Ramle

תגיד, 72 בתולות זה מה שעושה לך את זה?
מישהו עשה טעות בפרטים כלומר הם כבר לא בתולות והן בנות 72.

אודי, כיתה יא', רמלה

قل لي, 72 عذراء (حورية), هذا ما يحملك على القيام بهذه الأعمال؟
قد غلط أحد في التفاصيل. إنهن لم يعدن عذراوات ويبلغ عمرهن 72 سنة.

أودي, الصف الحادي عشر, الرملة

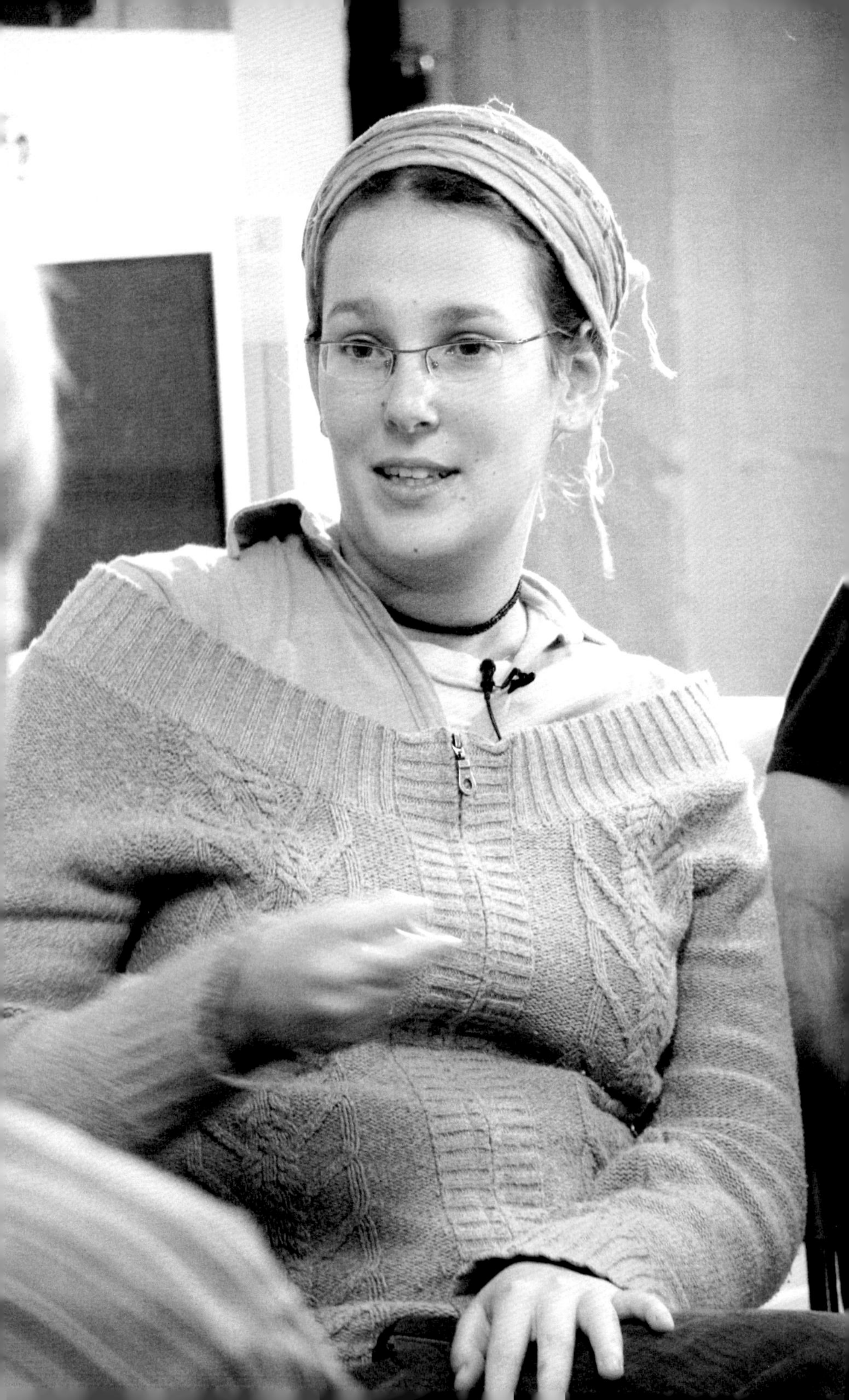

You must understand that it'll never end. Each side will hurt the other, and the other will respond by doing the same. We want a quiet world, a world in which children run around free in the parks and innocent people go out for a coffee and to restaurants without any fear. Listen, we're all people, even "cousins". We can manage together and co-exist. I believe it, even if you don't. You could give it a try…

Nina, 11th grade, Ramle

הרי בחיים זה לא ייגמר. כל צד יפגע בשכן, והשכן יגיב באותה פעולה. אנחנו רוצים עולם שקט. עולם בו ילדים יתרוצצו חופשי בגנים, אנשים חפים מפשע ייצאו לבתי קפה ומסעדות ללא שום חשש. תשמע, כולנו בני אדם, אפילו "בני דודים" אנחנו יכולים להסתדר יחד ולחיות בדו-קיום, אפילו שאתה לא מאמין. אפשר לנסות....

נינה , כיתה י"א, רמלה

.إن ذلك لن ينتهي أبدًا. كل طرف يصيب جاره, ويرد الجار بصورة مماثلة
نريد عالمًا هادئًا. عالم يتراكض فيه الأطفال في الحدائق بحرية, ويقعد الناس الأبرياء في المقاهي والمطاعم دون أي خوف.
إسمع, كلنا بشر, وحتى أبناء عام ويمكننا العيش مع البعض والتعايش, حتى إن لم تصدق ذلك. من الممكن أن نجرب ...

نينا, الصف الحادي عشر, الرملة

Every one of us creates an intricate network of connections around himself. Then here you come, out of the blue, and not only unstitch this amazing weaving of life, but tear, cut, slice, and ruin the whole fabric, without showing any mercy.

Elior, 11th grade, Sderot

כל אחד מאיתנו הוא עולם ומלואו, על אחד מאיתנו יוצר רשת סבוכה של קשרים מסביבו, ואילו אתה בא ביום בהיר אחד ולא רק שפורם את השזירה המדהימה של החיים, אלה פשוט קורע, חותך, קוטע, וגודם את הבד כולו ללא שום רחמים

אליאור, כיתה י"א, שדרות

كل منا هو عالم كامل بحد ذاته. يخلق كل منا شبكة متشابكة من العلاقات حوله. أما أنت فتأتي في أحد الأيام ولا تكتفي بفتق النسيج الرائع للحياة, بل تمزق وتقطع وتقص القماش كلها دون رحمة.

إلينور, الصف الحادي عشر, سديروت

www.israelikidsletterstoterrorists.com

There should be a television program or a site on the internet that will show how people live on both the Israeli and the Palestinian sides. Perhaps when we really know and learn about the other side we can succeed in solving the problem. Thank you.

Irit, 11th grade, Acre

צריכה להיות תוכנית טלוויזיה או תוכנית דרך האינטרנט שתראה את חייהם מ-2 הצדדים, מהצד הישראלי והמצד הפלסטינאי. אולי כאשר נדע ונכיר באמת את 2 הצדדים נצליח לפתור את הבעיה

עירית, כיתה י"א, עכו

يجب أن يكون برنامج تلفزيوني أو برنامج على شبكة الإنترنت يعرض الحياة من الطرفين، من الطرف الإسرائيلي ومن الطرف الفلسطيني. لعلنا عندما نعرف حقًا كلي الطرفين فنستطيع حل القضية.

عيريت, الصف الحادي عشر, عكا

There are Arab and Israeli children who want peace, who do not want wars and are trying, through different projects, to find a way to realize peace. If Arab and Israeli children are willing to compromise and realize a different reality, why can't you, too, try a different way? "He who takes one life ruins the entire world".

Shenhav, 11th grade, Acre

יש ילדים ערבים שמוכנים לשלום, שלא רוצים מלחמות ומנסים בעקבות כל מיני פרויקטים למצוא דרך להגשים את השלום.
אם ילדים ערבים מוכנים להתפשר על הכל ולהגשים מציאות אחרת, למה אתה לא יכול לנסות אחרת?
"אם גזלת נפש כאילו גזלת עולם ומלואו"

שנהב, כיתה י"א, עכו

هناك أولاد عرب مستعدون للسلام, ولا يريدون الحروب ويحاولون من جراء أنواع مختلفة من المشاريع إيجاد طريق لتحقيق السلام.
إذا استعد أولاد عرب لقبول التسوية وحل الوسط ولإحلال واقع آخر, فلماذا لا تستطيع أنت محاولة السير في طريق آخر؟
"إذا سلبت حياة إنسان واحد وكأنك سلبت الدنيا بأكملها".

شينهاف, الصف الحادي عشر, عكا

Perhaps you're doing it for personal reasons, maybe because your life is full of suffering, or maybe something else is wrong. But I want you to know that if a person meets problems in his life, he just has to try and overcome them. Even you could "repair" what you're trying to repair in a different and more useful way.

Pupil, 10th grade, Ramle

אולי אתה עושה זאת מסיבות אישיות , אולי כי אתה פשוט סובל בחיים שלך, או כל דבר אחר , אבל דע לך אם אדם פוגש בעיות בחיים שלו הוא פשוט צריך לנסות להתגבר על זה. ואפילו אתה גם יכול לתקן את מה שאתה מנסה "לתקן" בצורה אחרת , ומועילה יותר !

חניכה, כיתה י', רמלה

لعلك تعمل ما تعمله لأسباب شخصية, أو من الممكن أنك تعاني في حياتك, أو أي سبب آخر. ولكن, اعلم أن كل إنسان يواجه مشاكل في حياته وعليه أن يحاول التغلب عليها. وحتى أنت يمكنك تصحيح ما تريد "تصحيحه" بطريقة أخرى وأكثر نجاعة.

طالبة, الصف الحادي عشر, الرملة

There are many miserable people in the world and they are not committing acts of terrorism. I think you're a person who lacks feelings and a conscience. I want you to tell me how it is possible to kill innocent people who never knew you and did nothing to you.

Daniela, 10th grade Ramle

יש הרבה אנשים מסכנים בעולם והם לא הולכים להתאבד. אני חושבת שאתה בן אדם חסר רגשות ומצפון, אני רוצה שתגיד לי איך אפשר להרוג אנשים חפים מפשע?, שלא הכירו אותך ולא עשו לך כלום.

דניאלה , כיתה י׳, רמלה

هناك الكثير من الناس البؤساء في العالم وهم لا يريدون الانتحار. إنني أعتقد بأنك شخص عديم العواطف والضمير. أريد أن تقول لي كيف يمكن قتل الناس الأبرياء الذين لم يعرفوك ولم يسيئوا لك بأي شيء.

دانيلا, الصف العاشر, الرملة

www.israelikidsletterstoterrorists.com

I suggest that you should try to take a break from the terror business and relax. Go to some tropical beach, get into the water and keep going and going... until the water's a meter over your head.

Or, 11th grade, Ramle

אני מציע לך לנסות לקחת חופש מעסקי הטרור לנוח לנסוע לאיזה חוף טרופי תכנס למים ותלך... ותלך...ותלך....ותלך.... עד שהמים יעברו מעל לראש שלך.

אור, כיתה י"א, רמלה

نصيحتي لك أن تحاول الخروج إلى إجازة من الأعمال الإرهابية وتذهب إلى أي شاطئ بحر استوائي كان, وتدخل المياه وتمشي ... وتمشي ... وتمشي ... حتى تتجاوز المياه رأسك.

أور, الصف الحادي عشر, الرملة

Think about this... They'll never travel to see the world. They'll never propose to their loved one. They'll never get married and never hold their own baby. They'll never be smart, mischievous, or sweet. They'll remain among the fallen, forever. Who gave you the right to condemn these people to death?

Lee, 11th grade, Beit She'an

תחשוב על זה...הם לעולם לא יצאו לטיול מסביב לעולם. לעולם לא יציעו נישואים לאהובת ליבם, לעולם לא יינשאו וישבעו עולמים, לעולם לא יחזיקו תינוק, תינוק משלהם.

לעולם הם לא יהיו עוד החכמים, השובבים, המתוקים. לעולם הם יהיו חללים. מי בכלל נתן לך את הזכות לדון את האנשים האלו למוות?

לי, כיתה י"א, בית שאן

فكّر بذلك ... إنهم لن يقوموا برحلة حول العالم, ولن يعرضوا الزواج على حبيبة قلبهم, ولن يتزوجوا ولن يأخذوا رضيعًا في ديهم, طفلاً خاصًا بهم.
لن يكونوا الأذكياء والعفاريت والحلوين. إنهم يكونوا قتلى (شهداء) إلى الأبد. من خولك الصلاحية أن تحكم على هؤلاء الناس حكم الإعدام؟

لي, الصف الحادي عشر, بيت شآن

I have Muslim, Christian, and Jewish friends from all over the world who speak a lot of languages and have different beliefs. We get along great and I would even trust some of them with my life if I had to! I really hope that this letter will help you realize that it's possible to live together without violence.

Martin, 9th grade, Acre

ש לי חברים מוסלמים, נוצרים ויהודים מכל העולם, שמדברים הרבה שפות ומאמינים באמונות שונות. אנחנו מסתדרים ביחד מעולה ואני אפילו סומך על חלק מהם בחיים ומוות, אם אני אצטרך! אני ממש מקווה, שהמכתב הזה יעזור לכם להבין, שזה אפשרי לחיות ביחד בלי אלימות.
מרטין , כיתה ט', עכו

لدي أصدقاء مسلمون ومسيحيون ويهود من جميع أنحاء العالم يتكلمون بلغات كثيرة ويعتنقون عقائد مختلفة. العلاقات بيننا جيدة للغاية وأنا مستعد حتى أن أضحي بحياتي من أجلهم, إن دعت الحاجة! إنني آمل حقًا أن هذا المكتوب سيساعدك على الإدراك أنه التعايش هو أمر ممكن, دون العنف.
مارتين, الصف التاسع, عكا

Can you stop being a terrorist?
Be a normal human being?
Hope to see the new you soon?

Nazer, 9th grade, Acre

האם אתה יכול להפסיק ולעצור להיות טרוריסט ?? ולהיות בן אדם רגיל ??
נתראה בקרוב,

נזאר, כיתה ט', עכו

هل يمكنك أن تتوقف عن الإرهاب الذي تمارسه؟؟ وأن تكون إنسانًا عاديًّا؟؟
نزار, الصف التاسع, عكا

Israeli Kids' Letters to Terrorists

I believe that despair is one of the causes of terror. As long as there's hope for a normal life, choosing terror or supporting terror out of the belief that it will bring an improvement in life, is not reasonable. On the other hand, if you feel there's no hope for the future, or if you believe that your chance of dying young is high, and if through using violence there's a chance to improve your future, you must think it's more reasonable to support terror or join terrorist activity. I hope I gave you something to think about.

Shir, 9th grade, Acre

כל עוד יש תקווה לחיים נורמליים כפי שהם מוגדרים באותה חברה, הבחירה בטרור כדרך חיים, או התמיכה בטרור מתוך אמונה שהוא יגרום לשיפור החיים, אינה דבר הגיוני כל כך.
מצד שני, אם שוררת אמונה חזקה שאין תקווה לגבי העתיד, לא לקבוצה המדוכאת, ולא לגבי כל אחד מחבריה או שיש אמונה כי ממילא הסיכוי למוות בגיל צעיר הינו גדול,
ואילו בדרך האלימות יש סיכוי לשיפור העתיד, אז הגיוני יותר לתמוך בטרור או להצטרף לפעילות טרור.
מקווה שגרמתי לך לנקודות למחשבה .

שיר, כיתה ט', עכו

.أعتقد أن اليأس هو أحد أسباب الإرهاب
ما دام هناك أمل بحياة عادية, حسب تعريف المجتمع, فإن اختيار الإرهاب كنمط حياة أو دعم الإرهاب اعتقادًا بأنه سيؤدي إلى تحسين الحياة, لا يعتبر منطقيًا.
من جهة أخرى, إذا ساد إيمان قوي بأنه لا أمل فيما يتعلق بالمستقبل, ليس للمجموعة المظلومة من الناس وليس لأي من أفرادها, أو يسود الإيمان بأن احتمال الموت في سن مبكرة كبير, وأن عن طريق العنف يوجد احتمال لتحسين المستقبل, فعندئذٍ يعتبر دعم الإرهاب أو الانضمام إلى العمل الإرهابي أمرًا منطقيًا.
.آمل أنني عرضت عليك عدة نقاط للتفكير
شير, الصف التاسع, عكا

So, is your family getting money for your suicide? Do you think there's not a price tag on your life? Do you think your family doesn't care that they're never going to see you alive again? Before you do another thing like this, it's better to think two minutes before you do it...

Ana, 10th grade, Acre

זה שהמשפחה שלך מקבלת כסף על זה שאתה הולך להתאבד,
אתה חושב שיש מחיר לחייך ?
ולמשפחה שלך לא איכפת מזה שהם לא יראו אותך יותר בחיים ??
לפני שתעשה עוד מעשה כזה עדיף לחשוב שתי דקות לפני..

אנה , כיתה י', עכו

إن عائلتك تقبض المال مقابل انتحارك.
هل تعتقد بأن لحياتك ثمن؟
وعائلتك لا تبالي بأنها لن تراك حيًا أبدًا؟؟
قبل أن تقوم بعمل مثل هذا فمن المستحسن أن تفكر دقيقتين قبل ذلك...
أنا, الصف العاشر, عكا

In our Holy Bible, and surely in yours, it's a sin to murder. The more I write in this letter, the less I understand your line of reasoning, the logic behind the things you do, the lack of feeling. Help us stop the terror that has been ruling the world for years now. There are enough natural disasters and accidents that kill whole populations without people killing other people for unjustified reasons.

Shiraz, 11th grade, Dimona

בתורה שלנו, ובטח גם שלכם זה אחד החטאים לרצוח.
ככל שאני כותבת אני מרגישה שאני מבינה פחות את קו המחשבה שלך. את ההיגיון שמאחורי הדברים שאתה עושה, את חוסר הרגש.
תעזרו לנו לעצור את הטרור ששולט בעולם כבר לאורך שנים, יש מספיק אסונות טבע, ותאונות שהורגות אוכלוסיות שלמות מכדי שאנשים ירימו חרב על אנשים אחרים מסיבות לא מוצדקות.

שירז, כיתה י"א, דימונה.

إن التوراة التي نؤمن بها والكتاب المقدس الذي تؤمنون به يعتبران, بالتأكيد, القتل خطيئة.
كلما كتبت شعرت بأنني أفهم أقل شيء طريقة تفكيرك, والمنطق وراء أعمالك, وانعدام العواطف عندك.
ساعدونا على إيقاف الإرهاب الذي يسود العالم منذ سنوات طويلة. هناك كفاية من الكوارث الطبيعية والحوادث التي تقتل مجموعات كاملة من الناس, ولا حاجة أن ناسًا يشهرون سيوفهم نحو ناس آخرين دون مبررٍ كافٍ.

شيراز, الصف الحادي عشر, ديمونا

Retire from being a terrorist.
It's not good for your health.

Michael, 10th grade, Dimona

.תפרוש מלהיות טרוריסט. זה לא בריא לך
.מיכאל, כיתה י', דימונה

.أترك عملك الإرهابي. ذلك لا يفيد صحتك
ميخائيل, الصف العاشر, ديمونا

Israeli Kids' Letters to Terrorists

Tough childhood or what? What makes you kill/sacrifice yourself? Didn't you know we can solve things not only with violence, blood, and death, but also through rapprochement and peace?

Pupil, 9th grade, Dimona

ילדות קשה? אז למה לעזאזל אתה הורג את עצמך/ מקריב את עצמך? אתה לא יודע שאפשר לפתור דברים לא רק באלימות, דם ומוות אפשר גם בדרך של שלום והידברות.

חניך, כיתה ט', דימונה.

طفولة صعبة؟ إذًا, لماذا, اللعنة, تقتل نفسك / تضحي بحياتك؟ إنك لا تعلم أنه من الممكن حل المشاكل ليس عن طريق العنف والدم والقتل فقط. من الممكن أن يمكن ذلك بطريقة السلام والحوار أيضًا.
طالب, الصف التاسع, ديمونا

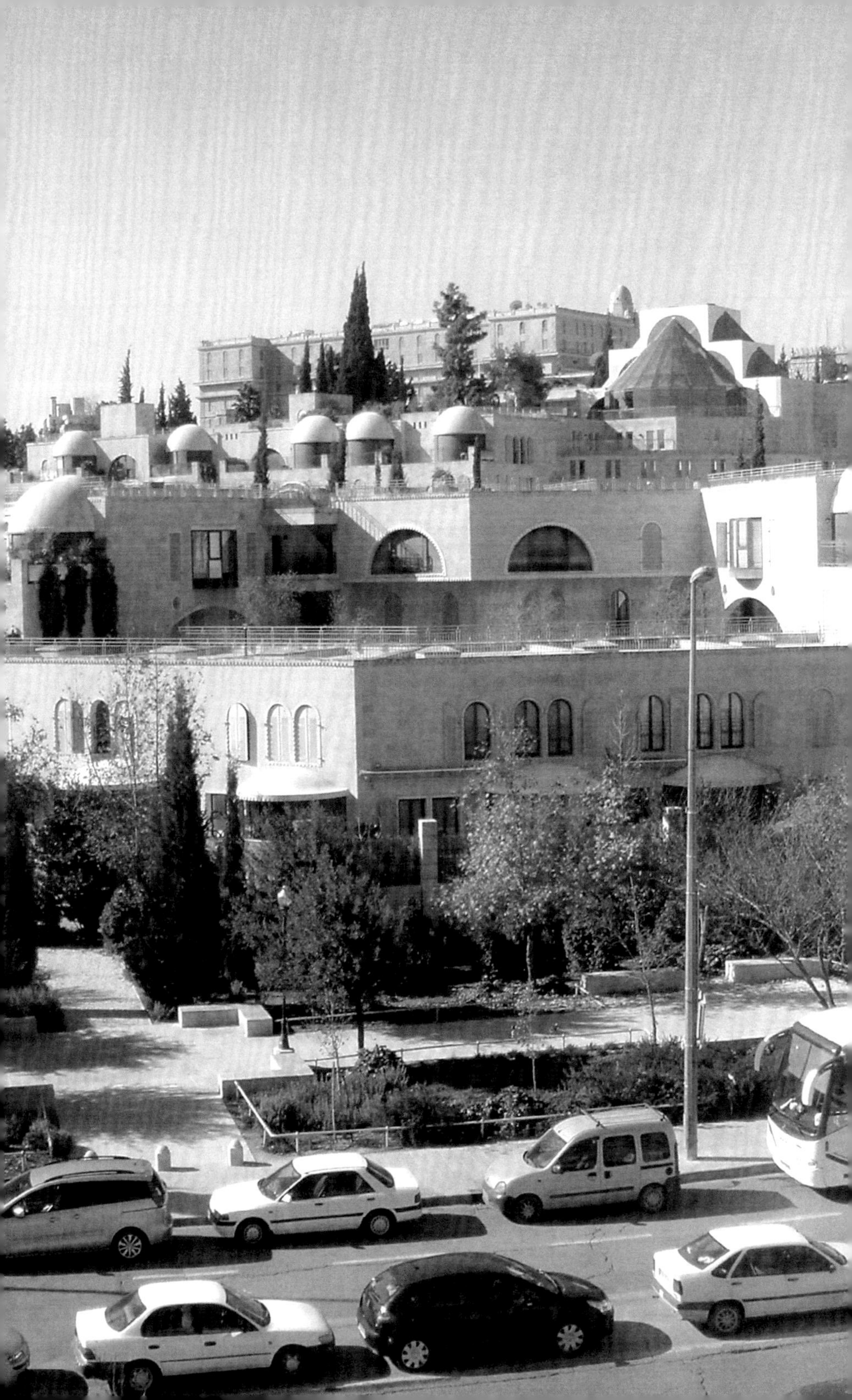

I suggest to you that you leave your life of terror and start a new life, without fear. Let the world manage itself without you!

Amit, 11th grade, Beit She'an

אני מציע לך לעזוב את הטרור ולהתחיל בחיים חדשים, בלי פחד. ושתיתן
לעולם לנהל את עצמו ולא אתה אותו!

עמית, כיתה י"א, בית שאן

نصيحتي لك أن تترك الإرهاب وتبدأ حياة جديدة, دون خوف. ودع العالم ييدر نفسه وليس أنت إتدير العالم
عاميت, الصف الحادي عشر, بيت شآن

www.israelikidsletterstoterrorists.com

I can't make you feel in this letter how much terrorism disturbs and hurts me!! I'd love to meet you face to face, and then, when you see my first tear, I'm sure you'll understand by yourself!! I hope to see you soon...

Yosef, 9th grade, Acre

אני לא יכול לגרום לך להרגיש במכתב הזה עד כמה הטרור מפריע לי ופוגע בי!! הייתי מת לפגוש אותך פנים מול פנים . ואז כשתראה את הדמעה הראשונה שלי אני בטוח שתבין לבד!!
אני מקווה שנתראה בקרוב..

יוסף, כיתה ט׳, עכו

ليس بإمكاني أن أجعلك تشعر في هذا المكتوب إلى أي حد يزعجني الإرهاب ويمسّ بي!! أشتاق جدًا أن ألقاك وجهًا إلى وجه, وعندئذٍ, عندما تلاحظ دمعتي الأولى فإنني متأكد أنك استدرك بنفسك!
يوسف, الصف التاسع, عكا

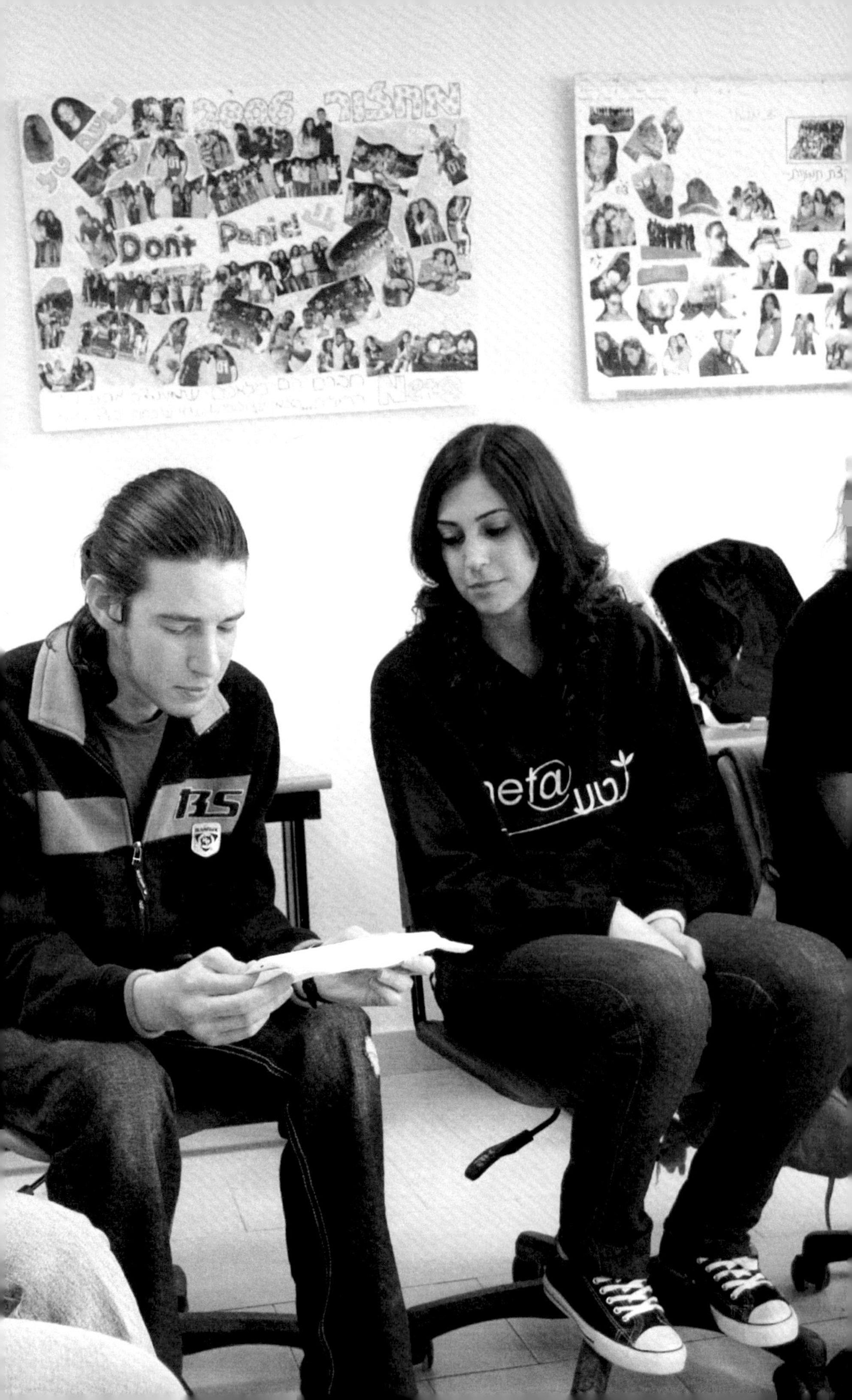
Don't Panic!
BS

By the way, as a fellow Arab, you need to know you're ruining the image of the Arab nation. Because of you, people are afraid of us and it's more difficult for us to fit into society. There's a beautiful life outside; you just have to look for it. Try to enjoy life, and if you have a problem with the place you live in, just move to another place. Good luck with your move!

Chenchen, 11th grade, Ramle

דרך אגב אתה הורס את התדמית של הלאום הערבי בעולם. בגללך אנשים מפחדים מאיתנו ויותר קשה לנו להשתלב. יש חיים יפים בחוץ רק צריך לחפש אותם. תנסה ליהנות מהחיים ואם יש לך בעיה עם המקום שאתה חי בו פשוט תעבור מקום.

חנחן, כיתה י"א, רמלה

على فكرة, أنت تشوه صورة الشعب العربي في العالم. بسببك يخاف الناس منا ويصعب علينا الاندماج.
هناك حياة جميلة خارجًا, يجب البحث عنها فقط. حاول أن تستمتع بالحياة وإذا كانت لديك مشكلة بالنسبة للمكان الذي تعيش فيه, فانتقل إلى مكان آخر.

حنحن, الصف الحادي عشر, الرملة

According to my understanding, you're committing terrorism so you can capture the state of Israel. So think about it for a moment—why do you need it so much? Muslims have 13 countries; we have just one small country. So if the land of Israel is yours, will it change anything? Will it bring a significant change? Just imagine that all the people in the world could live without wars, just living their lives.

Or, 10th grade, Eilat

לפי מה שהבנתי, אתם עושים זאת כדי לקבל את מדינת ישראל, אז חשוב על זה רגע- למה אתם כל כך צריכים אותה? יש לכם 13 מדינות, לנו יש רק אחד קטנה. אז אם ארץ ישראל תהיה שלכם, זה ישנה משהו? זה יגרום לשינוי משמעותי? תתאר לך שכל האנשים בעולם היו חיים ללא מלחמות, פשוט חיים את חייהם.

און, כיתה י׳, אילת

حسب ما فهمت, أنتم تعملون ذلك لتسيطروا على دولة إسرائيل. فكر لحظة: لماذا تحتاجون إليها؟ لديكم 13 دولة, وإذا ملكتم أرض إسرائيل, فهل يعتبر ذلك تغييرًا حاسمًا بالنسبة لكم؟ تخيل لنفسك أن جميع الناس في العالم كانوا يعيشون دون حروب, يعيشون حياتهم, لا غير.

أور, إيلات

People die all the time, of old age, of diseases, of natural disasters, of many things, so why do we need people to kill other people as well? A friend of mine was at the site of a terrorist attack and was luckily saved because they killed the terrorist first. He took a picture of that terrorist, a head without a body. Does it seem logical to you to die like this? For what? For what cause? How exactly can a parent send his child to die in order to kill other people? You live with that much hate? How do you justify your actions so that you can sleep well at night?

Tomer, 9th grade, Eilat

אנשים מתים כל הזמן מזקנה, ממחלות, מאסונות טבע ממלא דברים אז אנחנו עוד צריכים שאנשים ירצחו אנשים?
ידיד שלי שהיה במקום פיגוע שניצל במזל כי הספיקו להרוג את המחבל השני צילם את הגופה של המחבל אם אפשר לקרוא לזה ככה, ראש ללא גוף.
זה נראה לך הגיוני למות ככה? בשביל מה? למען מה?
איך בדיוק הורה יכול לשלוח את הילד שלו למות בכדי להרוג אנשים אחרים, עד כדי כך אתם חיים בשנאה?
איך אתה מצדיק את מעשייך בפני עצמך כדי לישון טוב בלילה?

תומר, כיתה ט', אילת

يموت ناس طول الوقت من الشيخوخة والأمراض والكوارث الطبيعية والكثير من الأشياء الأخرى, فلا نحتاج إلى ناس يقتلون ناسًا. صديقي الذي قد حضر مكانًا حدثت فيه عملية إرهابية نجا بأعجوبة, لأن الإرهابي قتل أولا. وقد التقط صديقي صورة لجثة الإرهابي, إن صح أن ندعوها جثة, رأس دون جسم.
هل من المعقول, حسب رأيك, الموت بهذه الطريقة؟ لماذا؟ لأي غاية؟
كيف يمكن الوالد أو الوالدة أن يرسلا ولدهما إلى الموت ليقتل ناسًا آخرين.
هل تعيشون حالة من الكراهية على هذا الحد؟
كيف تبرر أعمالك لنفسك, لكي تنام في الليالي نومًا هادئًا؟

تومر, الصف التاسع, إيلات

Israeli Kids' Letters to Terrorists

I am an Arab and a Muslim and I don't get it. Are you trying to prove to me that you're strong? Are you trying to scare me? I am telling you that you're strong and you managed to frighten me! You need psychological treatment. I don't want Gaza to suffer. I don't want the citizens of Israel to suffer. Terror results from misunderstanding.

Henadi, 9th grade, Ramle

אני ערביה ומוסלמית ואני לא מבינה. אתה מצפה בכלל שתשיג מהפעולות ? רציתי להוכיח לי שאתה חזק ? רצית להפחיד אותי ? אני לא רוצה שעזה תסבול אני לא רוצה שתושבי ישראל ייסבלו, טרור נובע מאי הבנות.

הנאדי, כיתה ט', רמלה

أنا عربية ومسلمة ولا أدرك كيف تتوقع أن تحقق أي إنجازات من هذه الأعمال؟ هل تريد أن تثبت لي أنك قوي؟ هل تريد أن تخيفني؟
لا أريد أن يعاني سكان قطاع غزة ولا أريد أن يعاني سكان إسرائيل. الإرهاب ناتج عن سوء التفاهم.

هنادي, الصف التاسع, الرملة

If you're bored, go to the community center, try to find something to do and get a life.

Sahar, 11th grade, Ramle

תקשיב אם משעמם לך למתנ"ס תנסה להעסיק את עצמך ותמצא חיים.

סהר, כיתה י"א, רמלה

إسمع, إذا انتابك الملل فاذهب إلى المركز الجماهيري وحاول أن تجد لك شيئًا ما تعمله وتجد الحياة.

ساهار, الصف الحادي عشر, الرملة

I honestly believe that you need to stand up and fight for what you believe in, but I guess that our definitions of "fighting" are different. There are many ways you can express yourself without killing people.

Matan, 12th grade, Ramle

אני בכנות מאמין, שעלינו להילחם ולעמוד מאחורי האמונות שלנו, אבל אני מניח שההגדרות שלנו ל"לחימה" הן שונות. יש דרכים רבות שבהן אתה יכול לבטא את עצמך גם מבלי להרוג אנשים.

מתן, כיתה י"ב , רמלה

إنني أعتقد حقًا أنه يجب عليك أن تقوم وتكافح لتحقيق ما تؤمن به, ولكني أفترض أن تعريفنا ''للكفاح'' يختلف. هناك الكثير من الطرق تستطيع من خلالها أن تعبر عن نفسك دون أن تقتل ناسًا.

ماتان, الصف الثاني عشر, الرملة

If you want to live in an illusion that the entire world is guilty for your miserable life, keep on doing so, but just know that nothing will help you in desperate moments and that hate always loses.

Pupil, 9th grade, Acre

אם אתם רוצים לחיות באשליה שכל העולם אשם בחייכם האומללים אז תמשיכו לעשות כך , רק תדעו שכלום לא יעזור לכם במצבים נואשים והשנאה תמיד מפסידה.

חניך, כיתה ט', עכו

إذا أردتم أن تعيشوا في وهم أن العالم بأسره يتحمل تهمة حياتكم البائسة, فاستمروا بأعمالكم. هكذا فقط تعرفون أن لا شيء يساعدكم في الحالات الشديدة, والكراهية تخسر دائمًا.

طالب, الصف التاسع, عكا

There are many people who lost much of their family because of terrorism. They didn't become terrorists, they built themselves anew and got over it-you, too, can do it! Do you sometimes think of what will happen to the family of the people you kill? Think about it... they'll only be sad and live with a hole in their hearts all their lives. What if someone you don't know perpetrated an act of terror in your country? If it happened to you? If it was one of your family? Now think again if you really want to do it to others.

Mor, 10th grade, Ramle

יש הרבה אנשים שרוב המשפחה שלהם נהרגה בגלל טרור. הם לא היו טרוריסטים, הם בנו את עצמם מחדש והתגברו- גם אתה יכול! למצוא דרך להתגבר ולחיות מחדש...
חשבת לפעמים מה יקרה למשפחה של האנשים שתהרוג? תחשוב על זה...הם רק יהיו עצובים ויחיו עם חור בלב כל החיים. ואם סתם איזה מישהו שאתה לא מכיר היה עושה טרור אצלך בארץ...
אם זה היה קורה לך? אם זה היה אחד מבני משפחתך?? עכשיו תחשוב אם אתה באמת רוצה לקחת את האחריות ולעשות את זה לאחרים.
מור, כיתה י', רמלה

هناك الكثير من الناس الذين فقدوا أغلبية أفراد عائلتهم نتيجة الإرهاب. فلم يصبحوا إرهابيين, بل بنوا أنفسهم من جديد وتغلبوا على أزمتهم – فأنت تستطيع أيضًا! إنك تستطيع إيجاد الطريقة للتغلب على ما مر بك والعيش من جديد.
هل فكرت أحيانًا ما الذي سيحدث لعائلة الناس الذين ستقتلهم؟ فكر بذلك ... إنهم سيكونون حزناء ويعيشون مع ثقب في قلبهم طول عمرهم. وماذا كان لو قام أحد لا تعرفه بأعمال إرهابية في بلادك؟
وماذا كان إذا حدث ذلك لك؟ إذا كان هذا أحد أفراد عائلتك؟ والآن فكر إذا أردت حقًا تحمل المسؤولية وعمل ذلك للآخرين.
مور, الصف العاشر, الرملة

www.israelikidsletterstoterrorists.com

I live in a town where both Jews and Arabs live together peacefully. I think that in the future we have to reach some compromises. As terrorists, you seem to always take everything to the extreme and see everything in black. Why do you have to take innocent people and kill them? Why can't some things be white or even grey? Try changing the way you look at things...we really can all get along.

Roy, 10th grade, Ramle

אני גר בעיר מעורבת, שבה חיים גם יהודים וגם ערבים
אז אני חושב שצריך בעתיד להגיע לאיזה שהיא פשרה.
לא חובה להקצין את הכול ולראות את הכול בשחור, למה לערב בזה את כל האנשים החפים מפשע שאתה הורג?! למה חלק מהדברים לא יכולים להיות לבנים או אפורים?
תנסה לשנות את דרכיך ולהסתכל על דברים... אנחנו באמת יכולים להסתדר.

רועי, כיתה י', רמלה

أنا ساكن في مدينة مختلطة, يعيش فيها يهود وعرب معًا.
إنني أفكر أنه يجب التوصل إلى أي نوع من التسوية وحل الوسط في المستقبل.
لا حاجة لننظر إلى كل شيء نظرة متطرفة ونرى كل شيء باللون الأسود؟ لماذا يجب توريط جميع الناس الأبرياء الذين تقتلهم؟! لماذا لا يمكن أن تكون بعض الأشياء باللون الأبيض أو الرمادي؟
حاول تغيير سلوكك والنظر إلى الأمور بشكل آخر ... يمكننا أن ندبر أحوالنا حقًا.
روعي, الصف العاشر, الرملة

Writing this letter helped me. It helped me understand a side of me that I didn't know before. Perhaps you, too, should write me a letter.

Rotem, 10th grade, Ramle

המכתב הזה עזר לי. הוא עזר לי להבין צד שבי שלא הכרתי. אולי גם לך כדאי לכתוב לנו מכתב.

רותם, כיתה י׳, רמלה

إن هذا المكتوب ساعدني. ساعدني على فهم وجه آخر خاص بي لم أعرفه. لعله من المستحسن أن تكتب أنت مكتوبًا لنا أيضًا.

روتم, الصف العاشر, الرملة

www.israelikidsletterstoterrorists.com

How can you tell a mother that she's not going to see her son anymore? That he's gone? How can you tell a child there's no Dad? That he's gone? He's not at work. He's not on a journey. Just gone. And how can you tell a child that her mother is no longer here? And that she won't be back. A small child, who saw only enough sunrises in his life to go to school, and from today on, there will only be sunsets.

Nofar, 9th grade, Eilat

איך אפשר לבשר לאמא שלא תראה יותר את הבן שלה. שהוא הלך.
איך אפשר לבשר לילד שאין לו אבא. שהוא הלך. הוא לא בעבודה.. הוא לא בטיול. פשוט הלך.
ואיך מספרים לילד שאמא לא פה. והיא לא תחזור. ילד קטן. ראה אך בקושי מספיק זריחות בחייו כדי ללכת לבית הספר. ומהיום יש רק שקיעות.

נופר, כיתה ט׳, אילת

كيف يمكن إخبار الأم بأنها لن ترى ابنها أبدًا. إنه ذهب.
كيف يمكن إخبار الولد بأنه ليس له أب. إنه ذهب. لا يوجد في عمله. ليس في رحلة. إنه ذهب.
كيف يمكن أن نحكي للولد أن أمه ليست هنا, وأنها لن تعود. طفل صغير. لم ير ما يكفي من شروق الشمس في حياته ليذهب إلى المدرسة. فمن اليوم فصاعدًا يوجد غروب الشمس فقط.
نوفار, الصف التاسع, الرملة

We suffer from the Qassam rockets. We have the killing and the pain, but not over all of the country. That's why not all of us are feeling all the suffering like Sderot's people, who are experiencing it on a daily basis. You are suffering, too, and your hatred is probably stronger than ours. We don't deserve to hate you, or you to hate us...it doesn't accomplish anything.

Or, 10th grade, Eliat

אנחנו סובלים מרקטות הקסם, אצלנו יש הרג ופגיעה, לא על בארץ, לכן לא כולנו חשים בסבל כל כך כמו תושבי שדרות החווים זאת כל יום מחדש. אתם סובלים כולכם יחד שמה בעזה, והשנאה שלכם כנראה גדולה יותר משלנו, לא מגיעה לנו לשנוא אתכם, או לכם לשנוא אותנו, אין הגיון בכלל בכל המלחמה חסרת התועלת הזאת, פשוט אין.

אור, כיתה י', אילת

نحن نعاني من صواريخ القسام. نعاني من حالات القتل والإصابات بالجراح. ولكن ليس في كل أنحاء البلاد. لا نشعر جميعنا بالمعاناة كما يشعرون بها سكان سديروت الذين يعيشون ذلك كل يوم من جديد. أنتم تعانون كلكم هناك في غزة, وكراهيتكم, فيما يبدو, أشد من كراهيتنا. لا يجدر أن نكرهكم أو أن تكرهونا. ليس أي منطق, على الإطلاق, بكل هذه الحرب العديمة الجدوى. لا يوجد أي منطق.

أون, الصف العاشر, إيلات

It's so painful to see a group of terrorists on television quarrelling over the responsibility for the terrorist attack.

Sandra, 12th grade, Ramle

כל כך כואב לראות בטלוויזיה חבורת טרוריסטים שמתנסים לריב על האחריות לפיגוע."

סנדרה, כיתה י"ב, רמלה

كم يؤلمني مشاهدة جماعة من الإرهابيين في التلفزيون يتشاجرون حول تحمل مسؤولية تنفيذ عملية إرهابية."

ساندرا, الصف الثاني عشر, الرملة

Life was so perfect, a family full of life; father and mother, son, daughter… who needs more than that?! All this was erased in a split second. Suddenly, because of a strong explosion in a bus, that son became an orphan for life!

Shukri, 12th grade, Ramle

החיים היו כה מושלמים, משפחה מלאת חיים אב ואם בן, בת ... מי צריך יותר מזה?! כל זה נמחק בשבריר של שנייה, פתאום בגלל פיצוץ כה עז באוטובוס אותו בן נשאר יתום עכשיו, ולכל החיים!

שוקרי, כיתה י"ב, רמלה

إكانت الحياة في غاية الكمال. عائلة مفعمة بالحياة: أب وأم وابن وبنت ... من يحتاج إلى أكثر من هذا؟ اوكل هذا – تم محوه بجزيء من الثانية, فجأة. وأصبح الابن يتيمًا, لطول عمره
شكري, الصف الثاني عشر, الرملة

Do you think that God/Allah would have brought you into the world if He didn't want you to live? Who's the person you think loves you most? Is He willing to give up on you so easily? Try to think how you'd like the world to look without you. In my opinion, it wouldn't be better.

Tamar, 12th grade, Ramle

האם אתה חושב שה׳/אללה היה מביא אותך לעולם אם לא היה רוצה שתחיה ?
מי האדם שאתה חושב שהכי אוהב אותך ? האם הוא מוכן לוותר עליך כל כך בקלות ?
תנסה לחשוב איך היית רוצה שהעולם יראה בלעדיך.
לדעתי הוא לא יהיה טוב יותר.

תמר , כיתה י״ב, רמלה

هل تعتقد بأن الله تعالى كان يسبب ولادتك لو لم يكن يريد أنك ستحيا؟ من الشخص الذي تعتقد أنه يحبك أكثر شيء ؟ هل هو مستعد أن يتخلى عنك بمنتهى السهولة؟
حاول أن تفكر كيف كنت ستريد أن يكون العالم دونك.
حسب رأي هو لا يكون أحسن.
تامار, الصف الثاني عشر, الرملة

I think what should be done is to give terrorists an ultimatum: that peace is on the agenda. When there aren't any results, then someone upstairs should put his foot down and start moving things in a different direction because if not, it [the terrorism] is going to continue for a very long time. True, it would be difficult and there are many who will oppose a change in a different direction, but...everything else has been tried. This problem has to be uprooted and that's it!

Moshe, 10th grade, Ramle

מה שצריך לעשות מבחינתי זה להציב להם אולטימאטום שעל הפרק עומד השלום
אם וכאשר לא יהיו תוצאות מישהו למעלה צריך לדפוק על השולחן ולהתחיל
להזיז עניינים כי ככה זה ימשך עוד הרבה זמן
נכון שזה יהיה קשה ויהיו הרבה שיתנגדו לדבר אך אין מה לעשות כי נעשה כבר
הכול.
צריך לעקור את הבעיה מהשורש וזהו.

משה, כיתה י', רמלה

ما يجب عمله, من ناحيتي, هو وضع إنذار نهائي لهم وطرح السلام كموضوع رئيسي في جدول الأعمال. إذا لم يتم التوصل إلى أية نتائج, فيجب أن تمارس جهة عليا ضغطا وتبدأ بتحريك مجرى الأمور, لأنه ليس من الممكن أن تستمر هذه الأوضاع مدة طويلة. من الصحيح أن سيكون ذلك أمرًا صعبًا, وسيعارضوا الكثير من الناس هذه العملية. ولكن لا مفر من ذلك, لأن كل شيء قد تم عمله.
يجب استئصال هذه المشكلة, وهذا هو.
موشيه, الصف العاشر, الرملة

Just imagine that the person who's most important to you was taken away from you. What would your life look like?

Pupil, 9th grade, Acre

...תדמיינו שייקחו מכם את בן אדם הכי חשוב לכם
איך יראו החיים שלכם?
חניך, כיתה ט׳ , עכו

... تخيلوا أنه سيُؤخذ منكم أهم الناس بالنسبة لكم
كيف ستظهر حياتكم؟
طالب, الصف التاسع, عكا

Israeli Kids' Letters to Terrorists

Peace to you man, though insane, different and strange, Who believes in somewhat different promises. A man who causes fear, pain, and suffering to people he doesn't know at all. He must be suffering, too, But he doesn't understand this.

Roman, 10th grade, Acre

שלום בן אדם אמנם לא שפוי אדם אחר ומוזר
שמאמין בהבטחות קצת שונות
אדם שגורם פחד כאב וסבל
לאנשים שכלל לא מכיר כנראה סובל בעצמו
אך אינו מבין זאת

רומן, כיתה י', עכו

مرحبًا بك, إنسان عقله غير سليم, إنسان آخر غريب
يؤمن بوعود مختلفة بعض الشيء.
إنسان يسبب الخوف والألم والمعاناة
لناس لا يعرفهم قطّ, وفيما يبدو, هو نفسه يعاني
ولكنه لا يدرك ذلك.
رومان, الصف العاشر, عكا

In my opinion, it's not fair that people can't feel protected and safe in their own home, in their own country. It's not fair that parents are afraid to let their children leave the house for fear of never seeing them again. It's not fair that hundreds of soldiers are killed and are not coming home.

Malkiya, 11th grade, Dimona

זה לא הוגן לדעתי שאדם לא יחוש מוגן ונוח בבית שלו, במדינה שלו. זה לא הוגן שהורים יחששו לתת לילדיהם לצאת מהבית מחשש שלא יראו אותם עוד, זה לא הוגן שמאות חיילים וחיילות נהרגים ולא חוזרים הביתה.

מלכיה, כיתה י"א, דימונה.

ليس من العدالة, حسب رأي, أن الإنسان لا يشعر براحة واطمئنان ويشعر أنه محمي في بيته, في دولته. ليس من العدالة أن الوالدين يخافان من أن يخرج أولادهما من البيت خوفاً أنهما لا يريانهما أبدًا. ليس من العدالة أن مئات من الجنود والجنديات يُقتلون ولا يعودون إلى بيوتهم.

مالكيا, الصف الحادي عشر, ديمونا

Terror is not the way! There is another way, and I think that the action of hurting innocent citizens who are unable to defend themselves is an act of cowardice, nothing else. Think carefully before you continue on the path you choose, and then your end might be different from that of your brothers.

Ben, 11th grade, Dimona

טרור זו לא הדרך! יש דרך אחרת ואני חושב שבעצם היותך פוגע באזרחים תמימים בלי יכולת להגן על עצמם היא מוגות לב ולא דבר אחר. תחשוב טוב טוב לפני שתמשיך בדרך בה בחרת אז סופך לא יהיה שונה מאשר אחיך.

בן , כיתה י"א, דימונה

إن الإرهاب ليس الطريقة السليمة! توجد طريقة أخرى. إنني أفكر أن إصابتك لمواطنين أبرياء لا يتمكنون من الدفاع عن أنفسهم تعتبر جبانة لا غير. فكر جيدا قبل أن تستمر بالطريقة التي اخترتها. لا تتغير نهايتك من نهاية إخوانك.

بن, الصف الحادي عشر, ديمونا

The situation in my country makes me very angry, and I've had enough! It annoys me that you hurt and kill people from my country. Today you can't get on a bus without being filled with anxieties and fear that perhaps you won't get off it.

Sapir, 9th grade, Beit She'an

המצב במדינתי מאוד מכעיס אותי וזה כבר נמאס! מעצבן אותי שאתם הורגים אנשים מהמדינה שלי
היום כבר אי אפשר לעלות לאוטובוס מבלי להתמלאות כולך בחרדות וחששות ואולי לא תצליח לרדת ממנו.

ספיר, כיתה ט', בית שאן

إن الأوضاع السائدة في دولتي تغضبني وأصبحت لا تطاق! إنني أغضب أنكم تقتلون ناسًا من دولتي.
لا يمكن اليوم دخول الباص دون أن تغمرك المخاوف, لعلك لا يمكنك الخروج منه.

سابير, الصف التاسع, بيت شآن

Israeli Kids' Letters to Terrorists

I understand your pain when a member of your family or relatives dies. I understand the grief and the pain that our soldiers cause you, but you have to understand that it hurts us as well. It ruins whole families. It's a pain that we suffer every day, at school, at work or in our daily life. After the workshop we had at Net@, I no longer have hatred for the Arabs, because I have realized that hatred is poison. It's a wound that never heals. With lots of understanding and hope for healing...

Rahav, 9th grade, Beit She'an

אני מבינה את הכאב שלכם כאשר מישהו מבני משפחתכם או הקרובים אליכם נפטר אני מבינה את האבל את היגון והכאב שחיילנו מבצעים לכם אך אתם צריכים להבין שגם לנו זה כואב. זה הורס משפחות שלמות, זה כאב שסובלים יום יום אם זה בבית הספר, אם זה בעבודה ואם זה בחיי היומיום.
השנאה שלי כלפי הערבים כבר לא שנאה כי הבנתי ששנאה זה רעל, זה פצע שלא מתרפא, פצע שלא יכול לעבור.
בהמון הבנה,

רהב כיתה ט', בית שאן.

إنني أفهم ألمكم. إذا توفي أحد أفراد عائلتكم أو قريبكم أفهم الحزن والألم لما يسبب لكم جنودنا. ولكن عليكم أن تفهموا أننا نتألم أيضًا من هذه الأوضاع.
ذلك يدمر عائلات بكاملها. ذلك ألم نعاني منه يوميًا, إن كان ذلك في المدرسة أو في العمل أو في الحياة اليومية. إن الكراهية التي أكنها لعرب لم تعد كراهية, لأنني أدركت أن الكراهية هي سمّ. جرح لن يلتئم, جرح لن يزول مع الكثير من الفهم,

راهاف, الصف التاسع, بيت شأن

www.israelikidsletterstoterrorists.com

Terror is a way of expressing the twisted ideas and ideals of people who adopted violence as a way of life. You won't get a state by terror or violence. I haven't heard about any peaceful reality bred by violence!

Eliran, 11th grade, Beit She'an

הטרור היא דרך להביע את הדעות ואידיאלים העקומים של אנשים שכל חייהם זה אלימות . מדינה לא תשיגו ע"י טרור ולא ע"י אלימות עוד לא שמעתי על שום מציאות שהחזיקה לאורך זמן ע"י אלימות!

אלירן, כיתה י"א, בית שאן

إن الإرهاب هو طريقة للتعبير عن الآراء والمثل العليا المعوجة لناس يملأ العنف حياتهم كلها. لن تحققوا هدف إقامة الدولة بواسطة الإرهاب وليس بواسطة العنف. لم أسمع بالواقع الذي يعتمد على العنف والذي يصمد ويطول مدة طويلة!

إليران, الصف الحادي عشر, بيت شآن

Israeli Kids' Letters to Terrorists

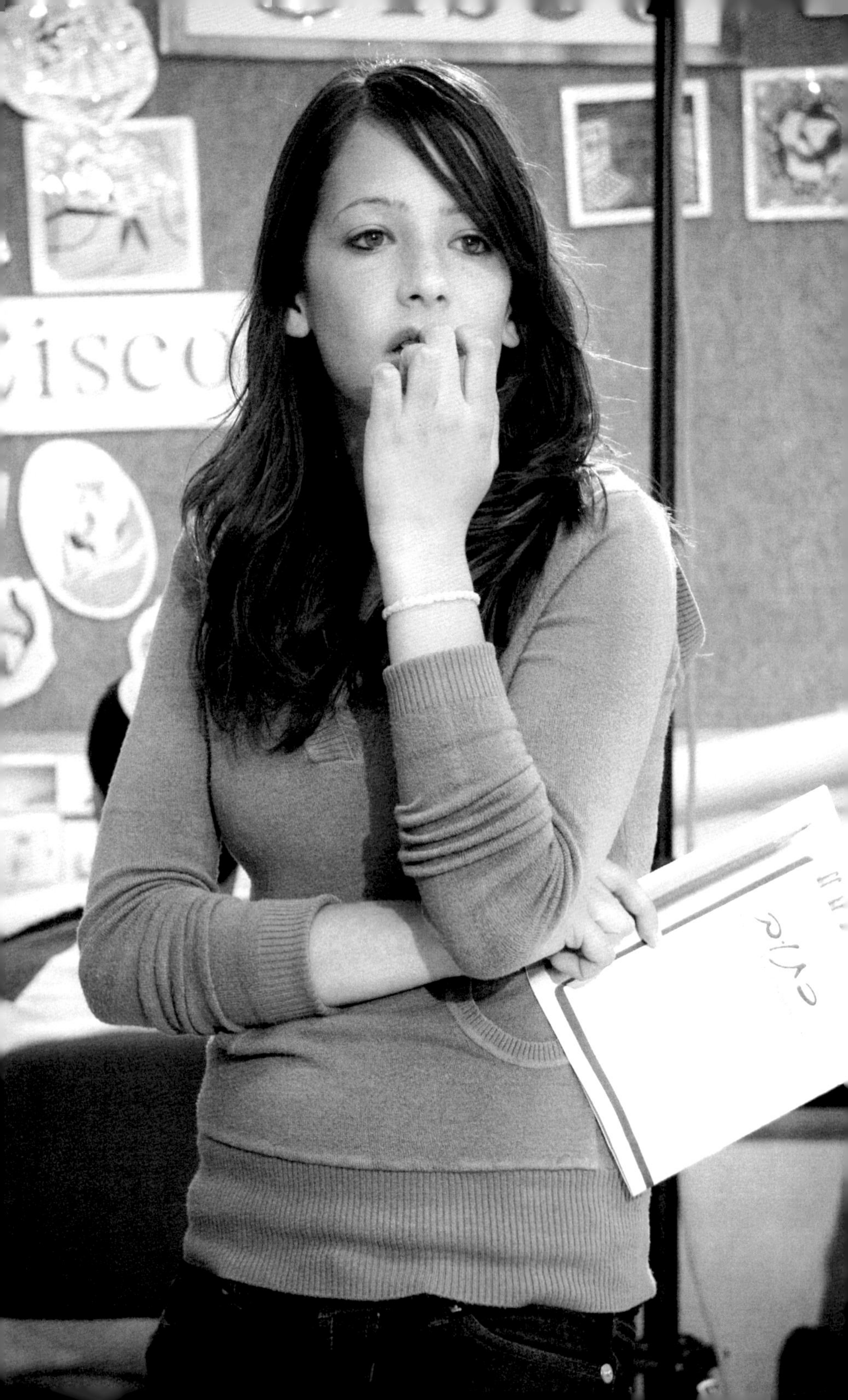
cisco

After every terrorist attack that you or your friends have perpetrated, I felt, and still feel, a heavy sense of distress, sorrow and sadness.

Mano, 11th grade, Beit She'an

אחרי כל פיגוע שאתה הוא חבריך ביצעתם אני הרגשתי
וממשיך להרגיש תחושת מעוקה גדולה מאוד, צער, עצב
ובכי רב.

מנו, כיתה י"א, בית שאן

بعد كل عملية إرهابية قمت بها أنت أو زملاؤك, شعرت ولا
أزال أشعر بشعور شديد بالغم والحزن والبكاء.
مانو, الصف الحادي عشر, بيت شآن

They say that "He who saves one life saves an entire world", and here you are destroying whole galaxies! Remember your family and perhaps... perhaps in the smallest place of good and purity that exists in all of us, you'll find another solution and stop your terrorism.

Mor, 9th grade, Ramle

אומרים שכל בן אדם שמציל נפש כאילו הציל עולם ומלואו וכאן אתה פשוט הורס גלקסיות שלמות! תחשוב שנייה, תיזכר במשפחה שלך ואולי... אולי במקום הכי קטן של טוב וטוהר שיש בכולנו תימצא פיתרון אחר ולא תעשה את זה.

מור, כיתה ט', רמלה

يقال إن الإنسان الذي ينقذ روحًا واحدة وكأنه أنقذ الدنيا بكاملها, وهنا أنت تدمر مجرات كونية كاملة! فكر لحظة, وتذكر عائلتك ولعلك... لعلك تجد, في أصغر موضع من الخير والصفاء الذي يوجد في كل واحد منا, حلاً أخيرًا ولا تعمل ما تعمله.

مور, الصف التاسع, الرملة

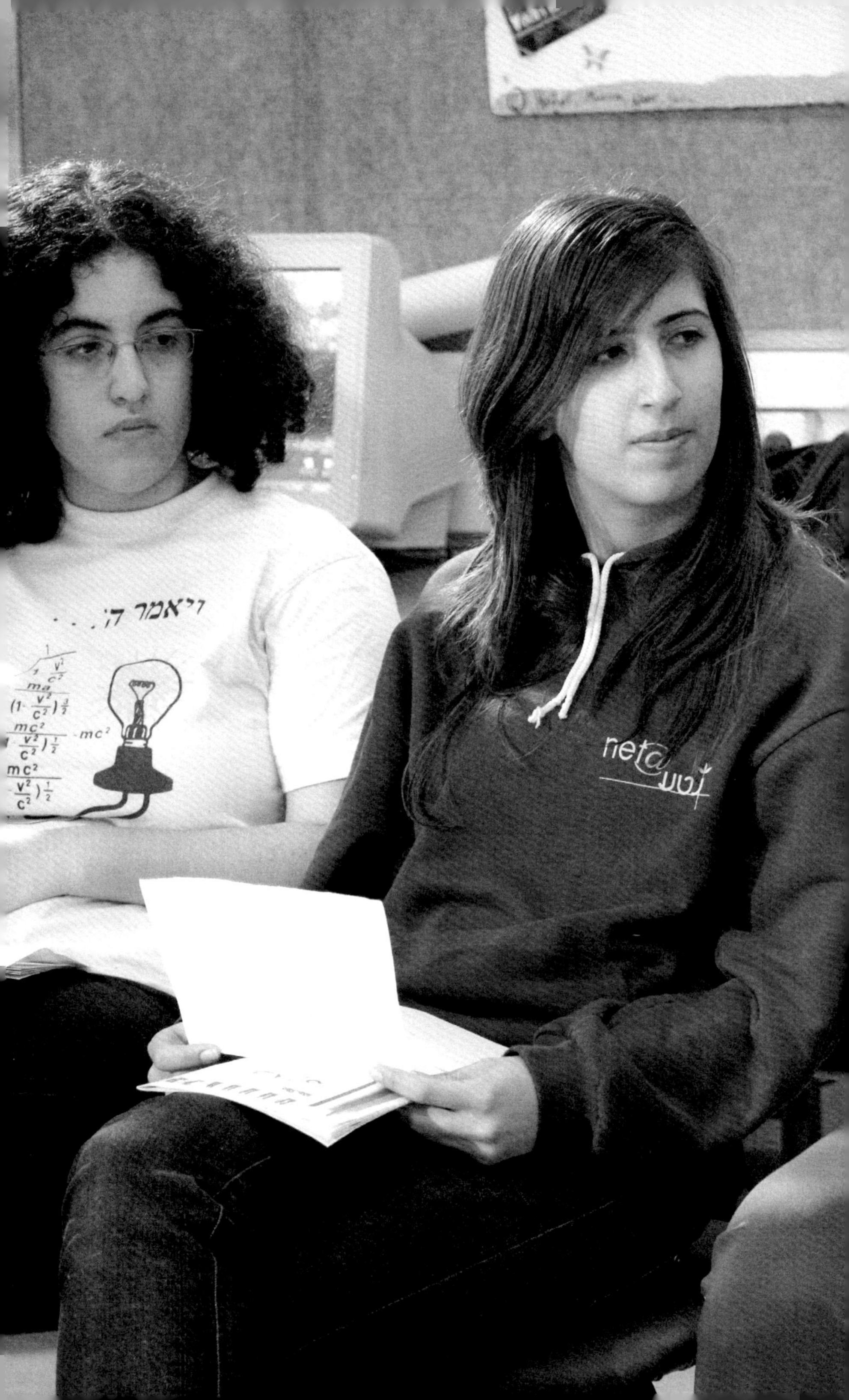
ויאמר ה
neta@

I asked my father if he was ever a witness to a terrorist attack. He said "yes". It was at graduation and terrorists threw hand grenades into the audience. His cousin was injured in that attack. Only then did I understand how close terrorism is to me. Close to each of us. My father was only a few meters away from not being here, from being a stone placed on the ground and people crying around it. Although we live in this bubble called Eilat, it's within us. Like a cancer, it is eating at all of us.

Nofar, 9th grade, Eilat

שאלתי את אבא אם הוא היה עד פעם לפיגוע. הוא סיפר לי שכן. זה היה בסיום של טקס סיום קורס ומחבלים זרקו רימוני יד לעבר קהל החיילים. באותו פיגוע בן דוד שלו נפצע. רק אז הבנתי כמה זה קרוב אליי. קרוב לכולנו.
אבא שלי היה במרחק מטרים ספורים מלא להיות עכשיו. מלהיות אבן שמונחת על הרצפה ואנשים בוכים עליה.
למרות שאנחנו חיים בתוך הבועה הזו שנקראת אילת זה בתוכנו. כמו סרטן שמכרסם בכולנו.

נופר, כיתה ט', אילת

سألت أبي إذا حضر مرة مكانًا حدثت فيه عملية إرهابية. ورد بالإيجاب. كان ذلك عند انتهاء حفلة اختتام دورة وقد ألقى إرهابيون قنابل يدوية إلى جمهور الجنود. وقد أصيب ابن عمه في تلك العملية الإرهابية.
وعندئذٍ فقط فهمت ما أقرب ذلك مني, من كلنا.
لقد كان أبي على مسافة بعض الأمتار فقط من ألا يعيش الآن.
من أن يكون حجرًا موضوعًا على الأرض ويكبي الناس حوله.
وبالرغم من أننا نعيش في هذه الفقاعة التي تدعى إيلات فإن ذلك في داخلنا, مثل مرض السرطان الذي ينتشر بين جميعنا.

نوفار, الصف التاسع, إيلات

Sometimes it's best to ignore the hatred and the animosity in the heart and act wisely to consider the good and the innocent. When using terror a person uses his power, not his brain.

Jessica, 9th grade, Ramle

לעתים עדיף להתעלם מהשנאה והטינה שבלב ולפעול בחוכמה . ולהתחשב בזולת ובטובים החפים מפשע . בטרור האדם משתמש בכוחו ולא במוחו ..

ג'סיקה , כיתה ט', רמלה

أحيانًا من المفضل تجاهل الكراهية والحقد الكامنين في قلبنا والعمل بحكمة, واعتبار الغير والناس الطيبين الأبرياء .. في نطاق الإرهاب يستعمل الإنسان قوته وليس عقله

جسيكا, الصف التاسع, الرملة

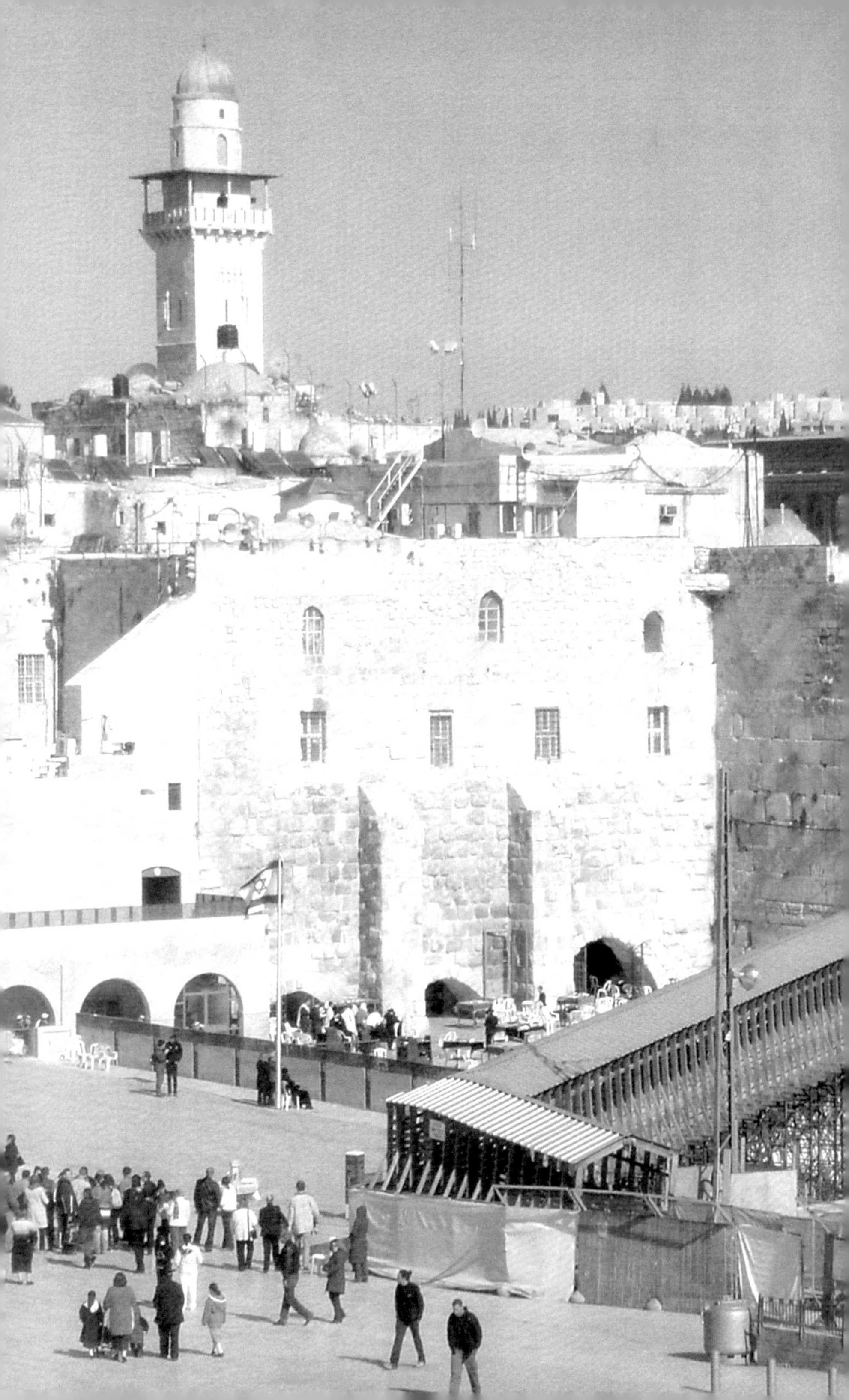

Do you want an idea for a better way to unwind? Buy a computer with a fast internet connection, play games on the network and kill as many people on your computer as you want! You will probably lower your stress level and enjoy it at the same time!

Elior, 11th grade, Ramle

אתה רוצה רעיון לדרך טובה יותר לפרוק עצבים תקנה מחשב עם חיבור מהיר לאינטרנט, תשחק משחקי רשת ותהרוג אנשים במחשב ככה אתה פורק את העצבים הכי טוב!!! וגם נהנה בו זמנית!!!

אליאור, כיתה י"א, רמלה

هل تريد أن أعرض عليك فكرة حسنة كيف يمكنك تفريغ الضغط النفسي. إشتر حاسوبًا مع اتصال سريع بالإنترنت, العب ألعابًا محوسبة واقتل ناسًا في هذه الألعاب. وهذه أحسن طريقة للتفريغ الضغوط!!! وفي نفس الوقت أنت تستمتع بذلك أيضًا!!!

إلينور, الصف الحادي عشر, الرملة

They say that terrorists have no feelings, but there's no such thing as a person without feelings. You must feel something, and I'd like to know what it is.

Meital, 11th grade, Acre

כמה שאומרים שטרוריסטים הם בלי רגשות אין דבר כזה אדם ללא רגשות , משהו אתה כן צריך להרגיש והייתי רוצה לדעת מהו.

מיטל, כיתה י"א, עכו

يقال إن الإرهابيين هم عديمو العواطف, ولكنه لا يوجد إنسان دون عواطف. إنك تشعر شيئًا ما بالتأكيد وأريد أن أعرف ما هو.
ميتال, الصف الحادي عشر, عكا

www.israelikidsletterstoterrorists.com

A significant part of the terror arsenal is the great publicity that the act receives through the media; but here we're using the media to get to you by publishing these letters. I know that this letter might not help much to stop acts of terrorism, but it's a good place to start; to increase our own awareness and that of future generations. I hope that my letter will help you understand the meaning of life and that things could be solved by words, not by violence and spreading terror.

Antonio, 10th grade, Ramle

חלק משמעותי מתוצאות הטרור הוא הפרסום הרב שהמעשה מקבל בתקשורת. אבל במקרה שלנו, אנחנו משתמשים בפרסום בתקשורת כדי לפרסם את המכתבים הללו.
אני יודע שהמכתב הזה לא יעזור לעצור את מעשי הטרור אבל זאת התחלה טובה להתחיל להעלות את המודעות שלנו ושל הדורות הבאים.
אני מקווה שהמכתב יעזור לכם להבין את המשמעות של החיים ואת העובדה שבעיות יכולות להפתר גם במילים, ולא באלימות ובטרור.

אנטוניו, כיתה י׳, רמל

تعار أهمية بالغة للتغطية الدعائية التي تحصل عليها العملية الإرهابية في وسائل الإعلام. ولكن في هذه الحالة, نستعمل وسائل الإعلام لنشر هذه المكاتيب.
إنني أعلم أن هذا المكتوب لا يساعد على إيقاف الأعمال الإرهابية, ولكنه يشكل نقطة انطلاق جيدة لزيادة الوعي لدينا ولدى الأجيال القادمة.
إنني آمل بأن هذا المكتوب سيساعدكم على إدراك معنى الحياة والحقيقة أنه من الممكن حل المشاكل بالحوار أيضًا وليس بالعنف والإرهاب.

أنتونيو, الصف العاشر, الرملة

Peace-it's such a small word...

Pupil, 10th grade, Ramle

שלום – זו מילה כל כך קטנה.

חניכה, כיתה י', רמלה

سلام – هذه كلمة صغيرة للغاية.

طالبة, الصف العاشر, الرملة

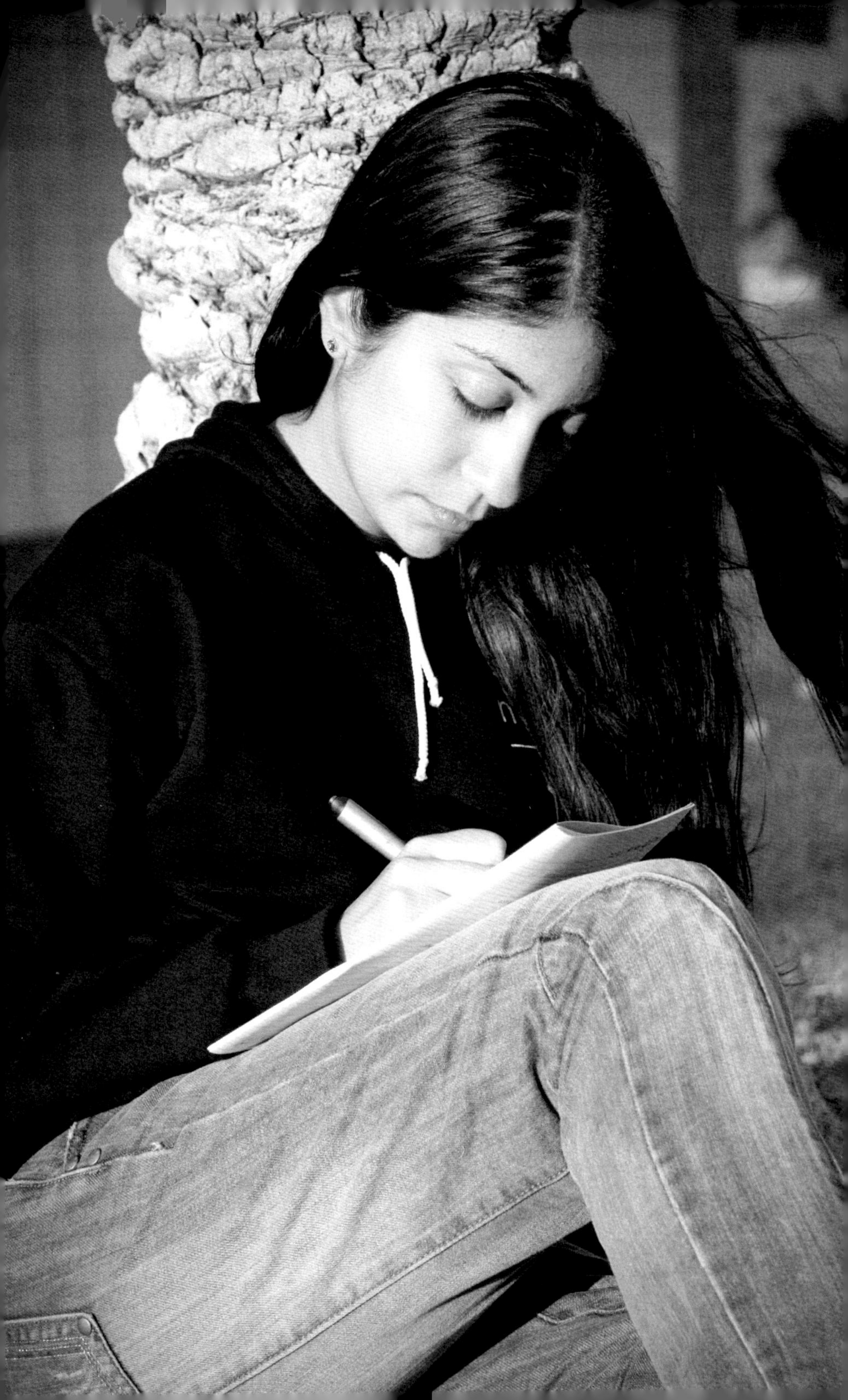

www.israelikidsletterstoterrorists.com

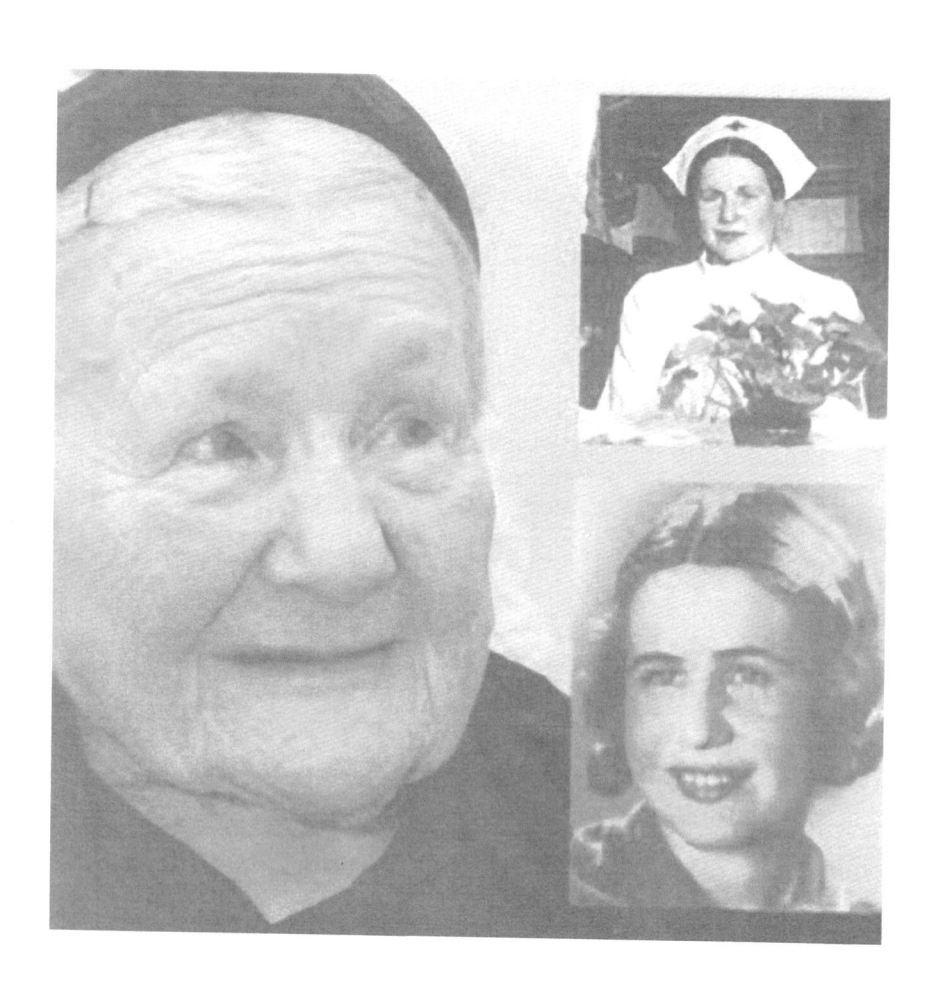

ANOTHER "THE STUDENT AS THE CUSTOMER" SUCCESS STORY: THE DISCOVERY OF IRENA SENDLER

"To Save A Child, is to Save the World"----Jewish Talmud

The true customer in education is the student. However, unlike in the business world where we know our success is determined by how well we respond to the needs of our customers, the customers in education are typically ignored. Most teachers "know" how their customers best learn, so they rarely ask whether or not their teaching methods are successful, and/or if they could be obtaining better results by changing or adding input from their students.

Miraculous things happen when we give the customers in education the opportunity to participate in the educational process. Our two books, KIDS' LETTERS TO TERRORISTS, and ISRAEL KIDS' LETTERS TO TERRORISTS are examples of the work that is done by students when they are respected and asked to participate in the creation of their own curriculum.

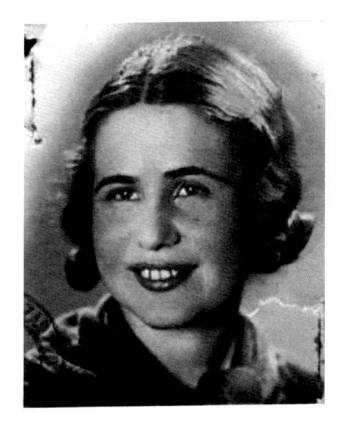

Another example of what happens when students are allowed to contribute to their education is the discovery of a future Nobel Peace Prize nominee: Irena Sendler.

As you will soon discover, the story of Irena is a remarkable one in and of itself, but it is made perhaps even more remarkable by the fact that few knew it! And, it can be argued that without the persistence and determination of four high school students from a small rural town (Uniontown) in Kansas, Irena's story would have died with her passing.

In the year 2000, more than 55 years after the destruction of the Warsaw ghetto, four high school girls from rural Uniontown, Kansas (population 290) were doing research for a history project when they stumbled upon a mention of Sendlerova (called "Sendler" by English speakers) in a 1994 *U.S. News and World Report* article that described "other Schindlers." Thinking that the magazine had made an error in crediting her with 2500 lives saved, the girls' teacher suggested that they do further research.

The girls found out that the magazine's figure was indeed correct, that Irena had saved more than twice the number of Jews that Oskar Schindler had. After they learned that Yad Vashem had recognized her in 1965 as one of the "Righteous Among the Nations," they began searching for her final resting place. Again, there was a surprise in store: Irena was still alive and living in poverty in Warsaw. They wrote her a letter. She wrote back. And a friendship was formed.

With information gathered from Irena, the girls created a play entitled "Life in a Jar" which they performed for a National History Day competition. After taking home numerous awards, the girls continued to exhibit their play around their community, passing around a jar at the end of each performance to collect money in the hopes that one day they would have enough to go to Poland and meet their hero.

In the early spring of 2001, John Shuchart, a Jewish teacher in a suburban Kansas City middle school, heard of the girls' play and invited them to perform for his class of middle schoolers. After the performance, Shuchart and the girls went out to lunch, where he grilled them with questions. After about 20 minutes, he realized that the girls needed to go meet Irena. When he asked them about this possibility, they said that they were planning a trip but needed to raise the money. He asked how much they had. "$180," they responded. "How old is she?" asked Shuchart. "91," they said. "She'll be dead by the time you raise enough money to get over there!" he replied.

Shuchart sat back, thought for a minute, and made the girls a promise. "You're going to go," he said. "Pack your bags. You're going to go."

And on May 22, 2001, the four girls, their teacher, and a number of parents and grandparents traveled from Uniontown, Kansas to Warsaw, Poland to meet a little 91-year-old lady who, according to the Jewish Talmud, saved the world twenty-five hundred times.

What the students discovered:

Irena Sendler was born in 1910 in Otwock, a town some 15 miles southeast of Warsaw. The child of working class parents in Warsaw, Irena was brought up with two guiding principles: (1) that people are either good or bad and; (2) if you see a drowning man, you have to hold out your hand. A Christian, Irena grew up in a diverse community, playing with both Jewish and Christian children every day after school. Irena never made note of someone's religion – her parents had not placed emphasis on it. If a person was a good friend, that was all that mattered.

In 1939, when Germany invaded Poland, Irena was a Senior Administrator in the Warsaw Social Welfare Department. With her government position, Irena was granted permission to enter the Warsaw ghetto regularly to check on the health of the inhabitants.

She knew that the future was dim for the Jews – that they were figuratively drowning and that she had to hold out her hand to as many of them as possible. Organizing a group of 10 friends and fellow sympathizers, Irena created a plan. It was organized, it was methodical, and it was very dangerous.

In 1942, the Nazis relocated some five hundred thousand Jews into a 16-block area that came to be known as the Warsaw Ghetto. The Ghetto was sealed and the Jewish families ended up behind its walls, only to await certain death.

Irena Sendler was so appalled by the conditions that she joined Zegota, the Council for Aid to Jews, organized by the Polish underground resistance movement, as one of its first recruits and directed the efforts to rescue Jewish children.

Every day, Irena would enter the ghetto and to try and convince Jewish parents to give their children to her. It was never an easy conversation; Irena could not promise a mother that her child would be safe. She could only promise that the child was doomed if left in the ghetto. After final embraces and rivers of tears, she would take the children and smuggle them out through the walls of the ghetto. She would place infants in carpentry boxes, carry young children under her coat, tell guards that the children had typhus, or hide them in ambulances that had come to pick up the dead. Some children were taken out in gunnysacks or body bags. Some were buried inside loads of goods. A mechanic took a baby out in his toolbox. Some kids were carried out in potato sacks, others were placed in coffins, some entered a church in the ghetto, which had two entrances. One entrance opened into the ghetto, the other opened into the Aryan side of Warsaw. They entered the church as Jews and exited as Christians. "Can you guarantee they will live?" Irena later recalled the distraught parents asking.

Once outside the walls, Irena, going by the codename "Jolanta," worked with a network of Polish families and convents to place the children. Children were concealed in Christian orphanages, raised by priests and nuns who sympathized with the Jews. Families would hide the children or adopt them as their own, giving them Christian names and teaching them new religious customs. As aiding a Jew was an offense punishable by death under Nazi law, these were very tense and difficult circumstances. Those that took in Jewish children lived in fear that an anti-Semitic neighbor might report them, and that the SS might come knocking at their door. In the blink of an eye, a good deed could cost them their lives.

Irena bravely, yet proudly wore the Jewish Mogen David armband into the ghetto as a sign of her solidarity to the Jews forced to live within the walls of the ghetto. She did everything she could to gain the inhabitants' trust, without which her plan was doomed.

The children were given false identities and placed in homes, orphanages and convents. Irena carefully noted, in coded form, the children's original names and their new identities. She kept the only record of their true identities on strips of paper put into three jars buried beneath a tree in a friend's back yard. Her objective was to hopefully one day remove the jars and go about locating the children. She felt it was important for the children to learn the truth about their identities, their parents, and their heritage.

Incredibly, the jars contained the names of 2,500 children.

Eventually the Nazis became aware of Irena's activities, and on October 20, 1943 she was arrested, imprisoned and tortured. The guards broke her feet and legs, but no one could break her spirit. Fully aware that she was the only one who knew the names and addresses of the families sheltering the Jewish children, she knew she had to withstand the torture, and survive.

Sentenced to death, Irena was saved at the last minute when Zegota members bribed one of the German guards to halt the execution. She escaped from prison but for the rest of the war she was pursued by the Gestapo and spent almost three years in hiding. She continued to oversee the daily operations of her fellow child rescuers. After the war she dug up the jars and used the notes to track down as many of the 2500 children as she could…but most of the families she placed them with either didn't survive the war or had been displaced and couldn't be found.

In 1965 Irena was accorded the title of Righteous Among Nations by Yad Vashem and in 1991, she was made an honorary citizen of Israel. On November 10, 2003, Irena was awarded Poland's highest distinction, the Order of White Eagle. And in 2008, she was nominated for the Nobel Peace Prize (she lost to Al Gore).

This story was largely unknown until the customers in education, the students, took charge and participated in a project of their own doing. They didn't give up. They did their research. They uncovered a "hero" of the Holocaust. Better late than never, due directly to their efforts, 55 years later, Irena Sendler's deeds were finally recognized.

Students CAN participate in the educational process; when they do, the results are as to be expected! After all, when the student is truly the customer, and the customer participates in the what, and how, and why and wherefore of education, why would we expect anything but positive results?

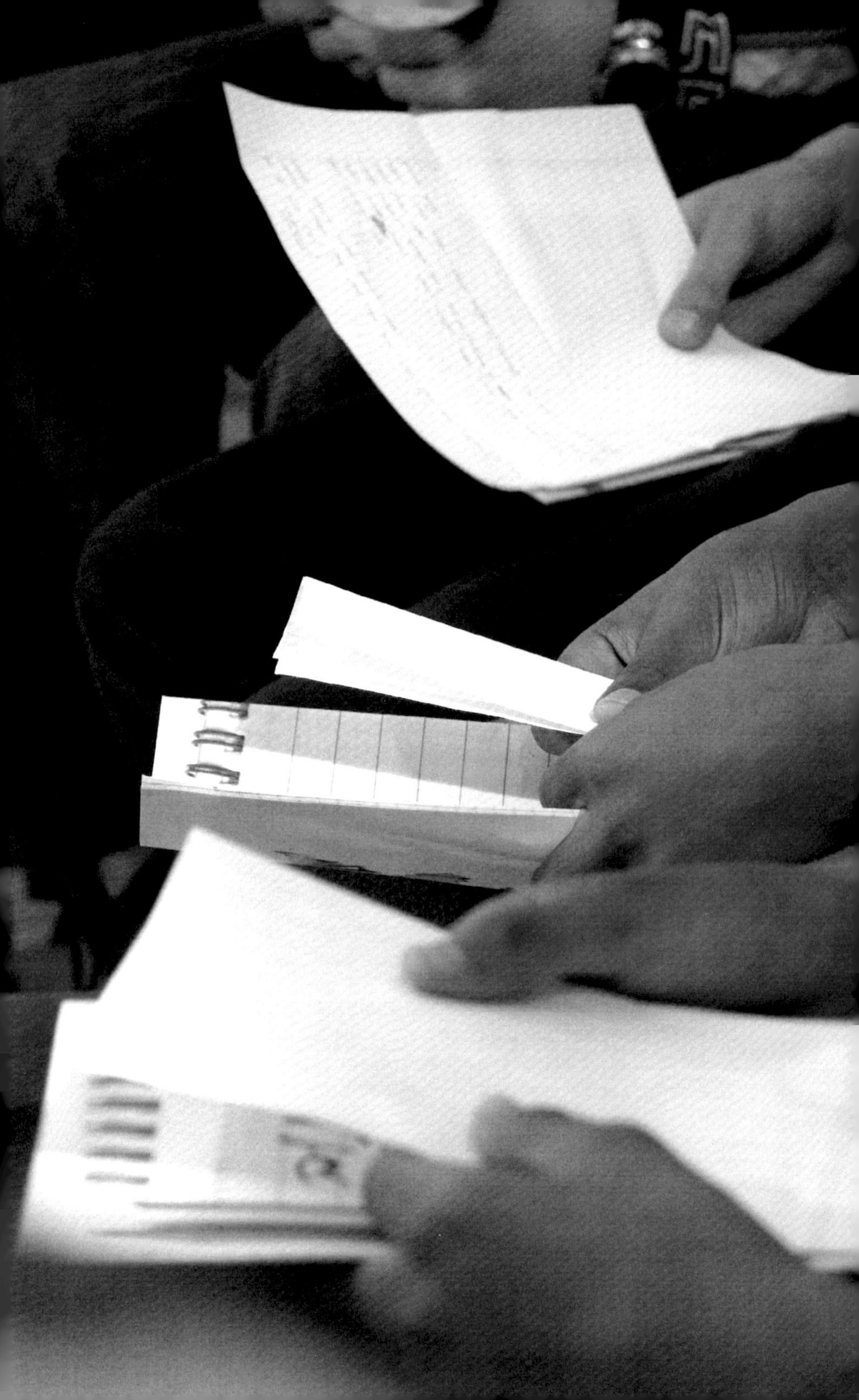

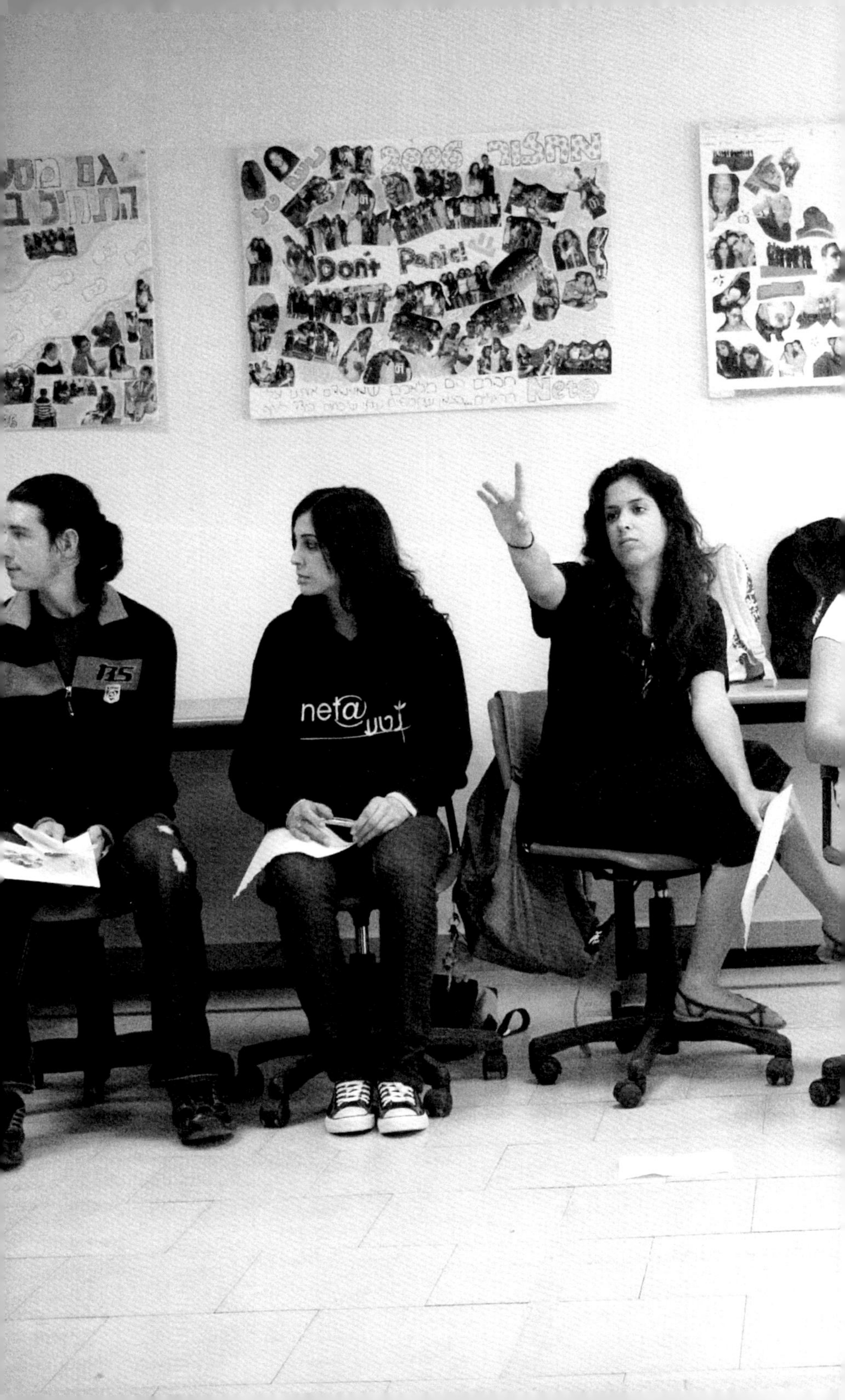
Don't Panic!
Net@
net@

כתוב

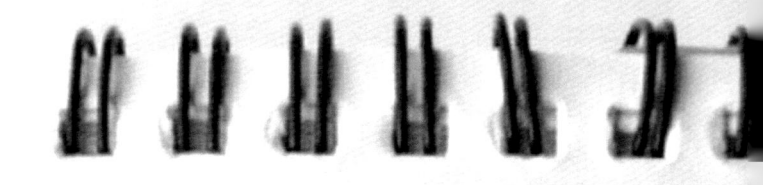

בני-נוער כותבים מכתבים לטרוריסטים

פרויקט ייחודי לבני-נוער: חוברת לחניך

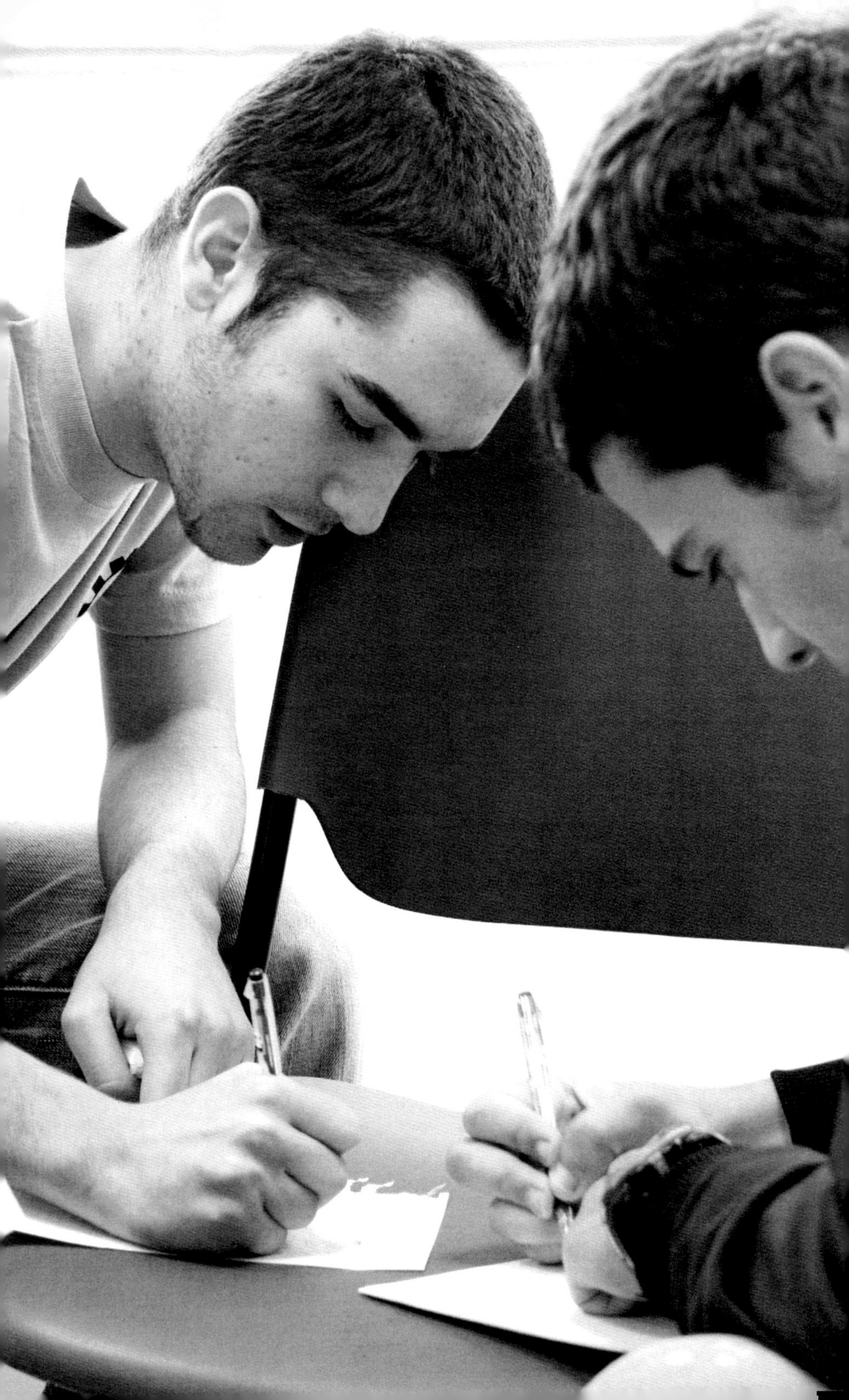

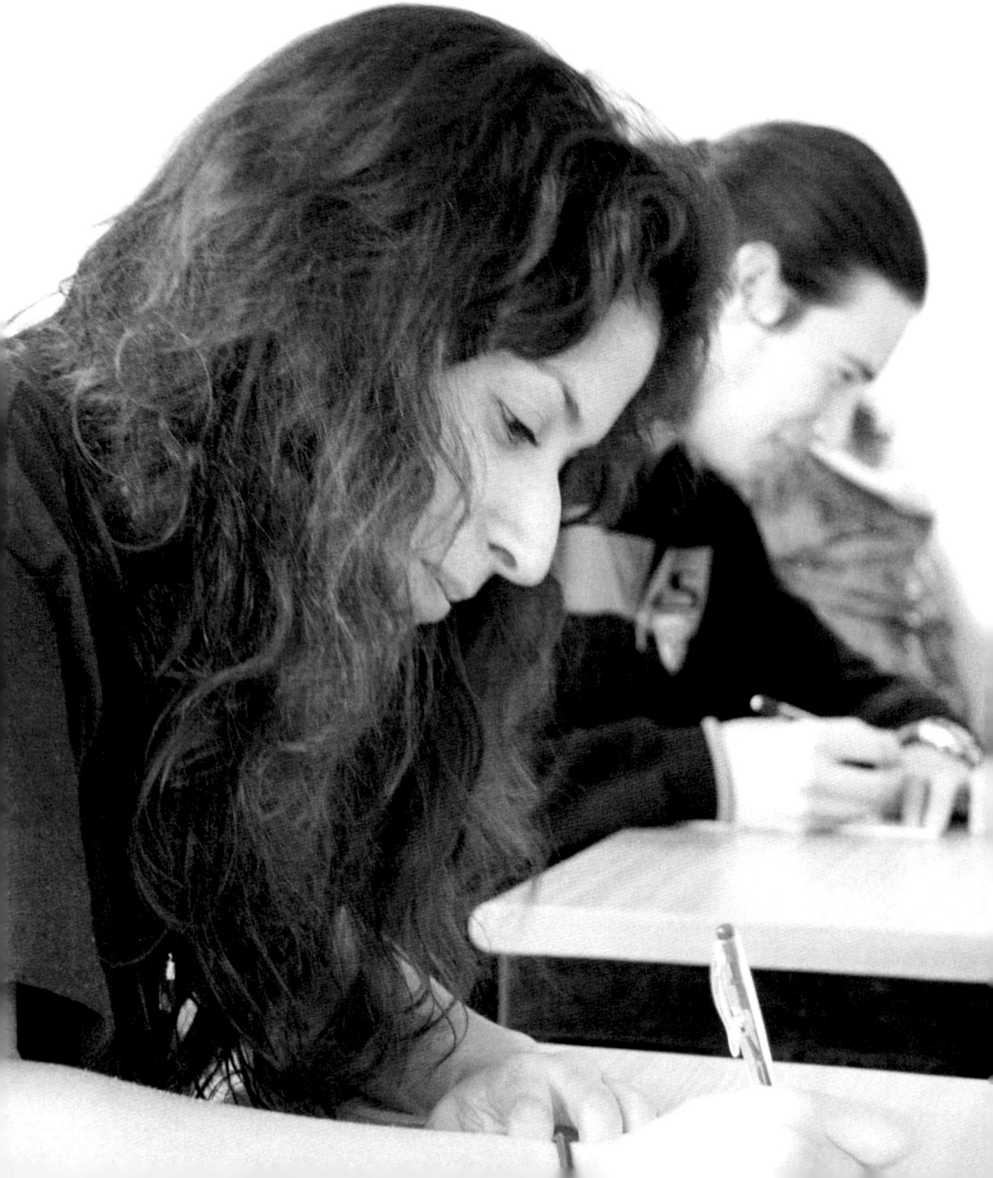

Acknowledgements

This book could not have happened without the educational partnership with Net@. This organization does a wonderful job teaching youth at risk the most important facets of the computer science world. From networking to loading more memory into a computer, Net@ prepares students for positions in the Israeli high tech industry.

The course on terrorism, WRITTEN, was created over two days with ten Net@ students from six different cities throughout Israel. The course was then taken by some 1300 Net@ students across the country. Letters were compiled, translated from Hebrew into English, and sent to me to be edited.

I had a great deal of help reading and editing the letters. Each letter was reviewed by no fewer than two people and in some cases as many as six different sets of eyes examined particular letters. A very special thank you goes to Steve Scearcy, Jonathan Dickson and Irv Gardner. Steve and Jonathan did most of the layout of the book, putting those pictures on the pages which best complements the students' letters, and much more. It was a very arduous task, but they did a fantastic job and the result is resting in your hand!

Irv Gardner latched on to this project and wouldn't let go. She tolerated my lack of organization as best she could, and she tirelessly reviewed every letter to make sure we didn't miss even one important sentence created by the students. I underwent shoulder surgery during this project and without Irv, this book would still be a dream. And of course, I give thanks to the people who gave of their time to read the letters: Alan Edelman, Diane Davidner, Carrie Shuchart, David Garrett, Michael Braudi, Paul Silbersher, Pat Henley, Stevie Shuchart, Todd Stettner, Rich Foellner, Scott Shuchart, Jack Bohm, Dr. Jennifer Gardner, and Joel Spangenburg.

Finally, the Israeli people who not only believed in the project, but devoted countless hours putting the logistics together, picking the students who would be creating the course on terrorism etc. Nir Lahav, Mor Karassin, Michal Nachum, Dafna Lifshitz, Eran Raviv and David Bernstein were super human in their efforts to make this project happen.

Acknowledgements (cont.)

My life has been enriched by knowing all of these people, but there are always some special people, people who reach out and touch your heart. Yochanan Levey, Todd Stettner, and Robert Socolof should receive a medal of honor for putting up with me. Yochanan (THE driving force behind this project for Israel...he wanted this to happen and didn't quit harassing the right people until he got the answers he wanted) and Todd (the Executive Director of the Greater Kansas City Jewish Federation) put up with me for a solid week in Israel. I can't think of a more difficult task. I complain about everything all of the time. The food, the bathrooms were especially frightening, Yochanan's tiny car (I always had the back seat since I'm a nobody). At one point they pulled over and voted whether or not to string me up and let me die in the desert, or just throw me out of the car and have the natives take care of me when I started my complaining. Calm heads ruled though, and they let me stay in the car (of course I had to pay for their lunch).

Robert Socolof, already swamped by his usual work load, found the time and energy to answer each of my phone calls. He found solutions for each problem as it arose. And, most importantly, he continues to believe in this project and is constantly sending more people to me who want to talk about our processes, etc.

And finally... Jeff Marks, my accountant, who once actually fired ME, the client! He eventually saw the error of his way and came crawling back. Then for an entire year, every Tuesday, at 4:30 p.m. Jeff came to my house to teach me Hebrew in preparation of my Bar Mitzvah (which I had at age 50 in 2000), probably my greatest accomplishment as an adult.

Harry Bosley, Mark Davidner, Richard Foellner, Harry Himmelstein, Shelly Pessin, Stewart Stein, and Larry Zimmerman have been supportive of me for a long time. Seldom does a couple of weeks go by without them calling me just to check in, to make sure I'm doing alright. For guys to care that much, well I'm blessed.

Acknowledgements (cont.)

Finally, my closest friend (well, really my second closest friend), Eric Talb. I've known Eric for 30+ years, and whenever the going gets tough for me, Eric helps to get me going. His unconditional support of me and all of my crazy projects makes the difference in my following through or surrendering. Eric never lets me surrender.

To my family, especially my children Scott and Carrie...they are without a doubt my harshest critics, never failing to tell me how to improve upon this or that. I know they understand my passion for each of my projects and I know they are never surprised with whatever I come up with next.

And to you, the reader: I hope you enjoy this book. It is an important book. It is a book about how young people living in a land of terrorism feel peace can be achieved. It would be nice if the world will begin to pay attention to their words.

John Shuchart
john@jshuchart.com
January, 2011

A Special Thank-You

An incredible amount of work went into creating and disseminating the course WRITTEN. We are all indebted for the leadership that the following people have so ably provided: Nir Lahav, Eran Raviv, Dafna Lipshitz, Yochanan Levey, and David Bernstein.

The following students along with Net@ and Tapuah staff are to be congratulated for their efforts.

Michal Nachum	Project Manager, Tapuah Organization
Mor Karassin	Educational Manager, Net@ Project
Yodfat Abulafia	Net@ Team Manager
Shani Cabra	Net@ Instructor
Koby Goren	Net@ Instructor
Idan Asian	Net@ Instructor

Students

Rasha Srour	Itay Ozer
Mathan Meir	Fakhry Dirbashi
Marina Izmailove	Galit Tasi
Maram Abu Sokhon	Udi Sasloni
Rotem Bar-Lev	Eden Gabay

It would be impossible for an international project of this magnitude to succeed without the efforts of many people. But, as we know, not all people, and not all efforts, are equal. It is unusual when there is one who stands above the rest, whose shoulders everyone stands "on" when the going gets rough. In our case, we had such a person: **Irvilene Gardner**.

From the moment she learned of this program, it has really resonated for her. Excited, passionate...she spent long, countless hours reviewing each and every letter (several times). She put more than 170 letters in a sensible order, so that our group of readers could review them in manageable groups of twenty. She made sure each letter had been translated into Hebrew as well as Arabic (not an easy task when you do not read or speak either). Most importantly, she kept each of us on track whenever it looked like we were going to stray (which was quite often!).

Irv was correctly convinced from the beginning that this would be a special opportunity for each of us who have had the privilege to work with these kids and to have read their letters. And, armed with that conviction, with a passion second to none, she successfully pushed this project to reach this project to its conclusion. A special person; a special thank you.

About the Editor

John Shuchart is an accomplished entrepreneur, educator and author whose business experience ultimately led him to focus on students as the true customers in education. *Kids' Letters to Terrorists* and *Israeli Kids' Letters To Terrorists* are both outgrowths of this philosophy.

He began his career teaching middle school Ancient and American history in St. Louis, Mo., following graduation from Michigan State University. During the summer he worked for his father training agents in the insurance business. He decided to remain in the business after a parent of a developmentally-disabled child challenged him to persuade the insurance industry to underwrite life insurance on disabled children. During his nearly 30 years in the business, he not only succeeded creating life insurance products for developmentally disabled children, he also developed new methods to mass market insurance.

John returned in 2000 to teach American history to eighth graders. Shuchart believes that the true customers in education are the students. But, unlike in the business world, most professional educators don't value their customers' opinions. And so, curriculum are set and teaching methods adopted without any input from the customer.

The answer for John was to create a course which would help teenagers get in touch with their feelings. The course AFTER™ was created for young teenagers in America. This led to the book, *Kids' Letters to Terrorists*.

John partnered with the Jewish Agency for Israel and the Greater Kansas City Jewish Federation to create a course on terrorism with Israeli students. He also played a crucial role in the discovery of a forgotten Holocaust hero, the late Irena Sendler, whom he had the privilege of meeting in Warsaw, Poland.

John is married to his pre-kindergarten sweetheart, a clinical social worker, and together they have two grown children and a grandchild on the way.

Students' Home Cities

The course, WRITTEN, was implemented in cities throughout Israel. As a result, the students participating had all had differing experiences with terrorism. Some had experienced recent attacks in their towns, while others had never been direct victims.

Here is a synopsis of terrorist activities in some of the cities at the time of this publication.

EILAT
The most southern city in Israel, Eilat is a city for tourists. It is a beautiful resort and important Israeli port located on the tip of the Red Sea. The city is usually very peaceful, but has experienced some terrorism, with one incident claiming the lives of three people. Many students from Eilat express more anger than students from other cities.

Dimona
A city in the Negev, some 20 miles west of the Dead Sea. Dimona has experienced at least one major terrorist attack where 38 people were injured, and one was killed. Students from Dimona have mixed feelings of anger, frustration, and hope in regards to the terrorist activities.

Sderot
In the western Negev, the city has been the frequent target of Qassam rocket attacks launched primarily by Hamas from the Gaza Strip. The rockets, although very inaccurate, have caused significant damage not just to property, but to the Israeli psyche. Many Israelis have left the city for safer areas. Students from this city tend to be very affected by the terrorism. They tend to want to find solutions so that the terrorism will cease.

Ramle
In central Israel, the city has a mixed Arab-Jewish population. Many of the students quoted in this book express a degree of empathy (but not agreement) towards the terrorists. They try very hard to understand every point of view.

Beit She'an
Situated in the north district, this city is in close proximity to the Arab nation of Jordan. Rarely faced with acts of terrorism, the city is almost exclusively Jewish.

Acre
Situated in the Western Galilee in the northern district, the city is of mixed population of Arabs, Christians, and Jews. Students from Acre seem to be able to express their fears and feelings about terrorism. Some of their quotes will really resonate with the reader.

Guest Speaker Opportunities

Mr. Shuchart has created a 45 minute dynamic presentation which he presents to audiences world-wide. The presentation is about the incredible results which occur when students are encouraged to participate in the educational process. Mr. Shuchart believes that the customer in education is the student and as such, deserves to be listened to. Coupled with the incredible story of **Irena Sendler** (whom he has met and is writing a biography on her), Mr. Shuchart shares with your audience how Sendler was discovered: four students from a small town in Kansas found out she had saved 2500 children from certain death in the Warsaw Ghetto...and that almost nobody had ever heard of her. It was the tenacity of the students (they were told to drop their search) that produced this incredible find. From almost total obscurity, Irena ended up being nominated for a Nobel Peace Prize in 2008. There is rarely a dry eye in the audience as they learn of the unbelievable commitment Irena had to saving Jewish children.

For more information on selling books as a fund raiser, or for reserving Mr. Shuchart for a presentation, please contact us.

John Shuchart
913.485.3336
john@jshuchart.com

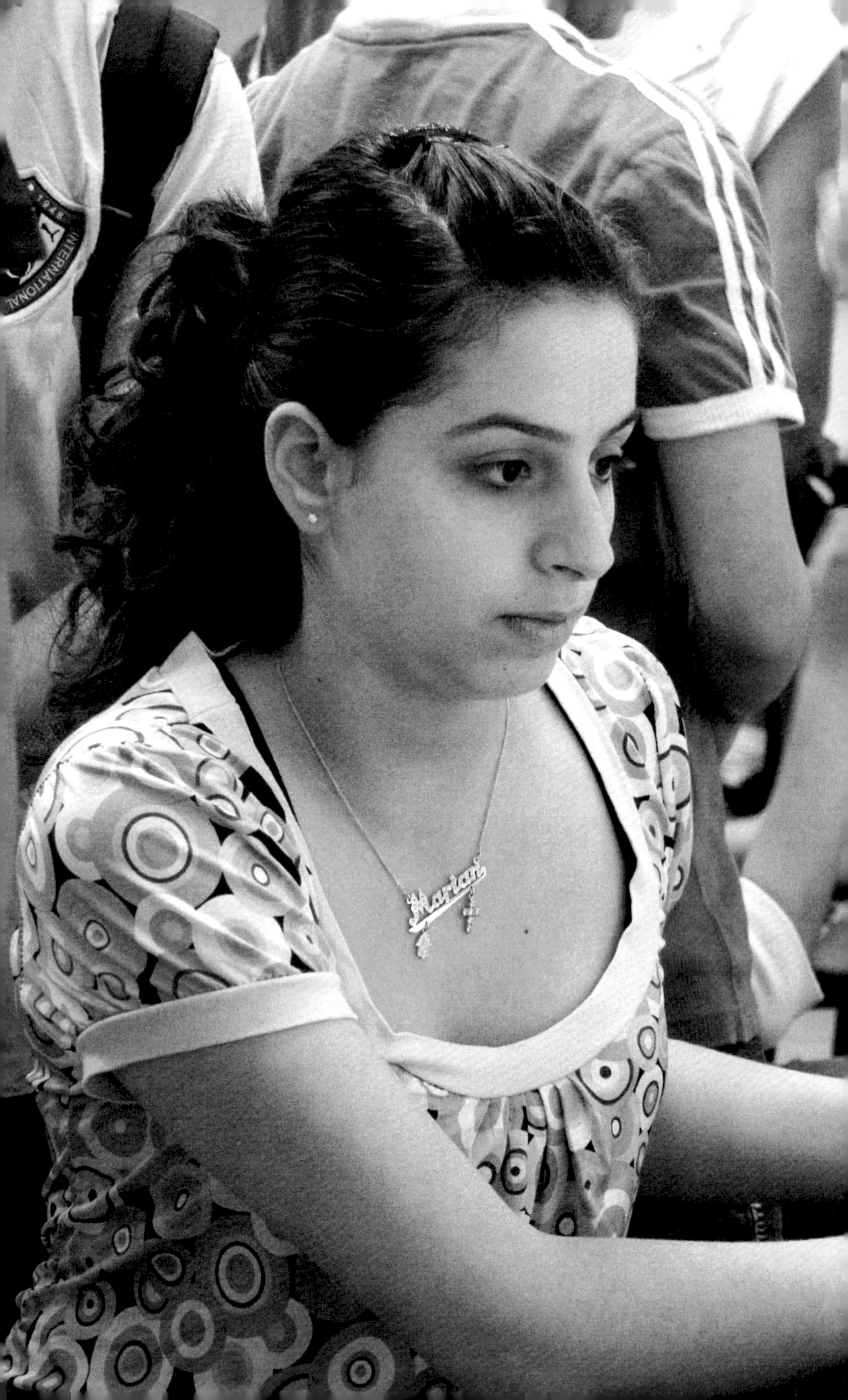

INTERNATIONAL

Notes

Notes

Notes